# MANIFESTATION JOURNAL

Instagram

@limitlessabundance_official

info@limitlessabundanceofficial.com

@limitlessabundance

# MANIFESTATION

So how do we, as black men prosper? It appears like every force in the world is working against us.

First, acknowledge your spiritual nature and connect with the beyond. Know that everything is happening for a reason and all things are good. No matter the religion, this is called faith. A perspective of pessimism towards life will only limit your possibilities.

Next empower yourself and begin a deprogramming of your mind. Leave the oppressor and oppressed mentality behind and become a sovereign being, unhindered by any force which attempts to restrain you. You are a pillar of strength and a force of creation. One who considers themselves oppressed or powerless, becomes oppressed and powerless. This is an understanding based on the principle that "everything is mind". It will take time as the brainwashing runs deep and I recommend meditations and books to assist in this process. Consistency is key.

Environment should be the next step. Look at where you want to go and look at the things which you allow and invite into your life which are counterintuitive to get there. You cannot be a top professional athlete with a smoking addiction. You cannot be a wealthy man with a gambling addiction. There are often many things which will actually block or hinder your energetic movement or expansion. This does not mean begin cutting out all pleasure and delete half of your friends. This refers only to those things which are directly counterintuitive, and thus harmful.

Discipline and focus. Now the mind is empowered and ready for movement- like a car with a full tank. The environment is perfectly suitable and accommodating for your dreams, like an unfurnished room. Many people at this point then expect the universe to magically do all the work for us. Not quite.

Now you must commit yourself to action which works towards the dream and you must be consistent. Remember you have already empowered yourself, so at this point it is nothing more than attention and consistency. If you do it every single day, focused on where you want to go, it will come. Imagine driving a car, this daily practice is like putting yourself in cruise control. If you want to accelerate, devote more work to it, however do not think you have to obsessively spend every second on it. Patience and consistency is far more reliable than intensity and overworking as the human body and mind can only do so much for so long.

You do not need to fight tooth and nail to get to where you want to go, just be committed, consistent and avoid getting too distracted.

Do this and daily life will, with time, manifest exactly what you desire.

The black man has a responsibility to not only do this, but teach those who come after. The more of us that do this, the greater we all become as a whole. In this way we will eventually rebuild and prosper as the empowered community we were always destined to be.

# BLACK MEN AND SPIRITUALITY

The black experience is unique in that it is a single shared experience and also a subjective and varied experience depending on individual circumstance. Those of us who are of African descent have a unique role and position in this world, one which is by no means designed to be easy.

Black consciousness is an interesting phenomenon as it is inherently tuned to spirituality. This of course historically has been used against us through missionaries and brainwashing however is still in any circumstance a virtue.

So how may the black man achieve greatness? It will require a strength unique to our plight. Black spirituality and empowerment requires an overcoming of adversity in nearly all cases. This is a consequence of where the African has always been placed in the global "pecking order".

The single most important thing to recognize is that, greatness and growth may only come by an overcoming of our limitations and weakness. It is easy for us to submit to an understanding that we are destined for less and even easier to submit to a mentality of bitterness. The outer reality, no matter the color or creed, directly corresponds to the inner environment. This is the core of modern spiritual understanding.

The African experience is a spiritual one, both historically and in our present day. In an increasingly secular world, it seems the black demographic plays a significant role in maintaining the relevance of spirituality and higher seeking. This dates back to before globalization and the transatlantic slave trade, when tribal pagan religions were standard practice on the African continent. This has not changed in spirit but has been remoulded in form into what we understand as institutional religions. This began as early as the 16th century. While we can get caught up in the politics of who worships what and why, the most important consideration here is the receptivity of Africans to spirituality and how this has been retained even today.

When we refer to spirituality, what we mean is a sensitivity to higher truth or guidance. We may call this intuition and is a subtle awareness of the unknown. It is thus quite unlikely you will see a huge wave of atheism take over the black population, as it would feel counterintuitive to what we already understand without realizing.

Those who close themselves off to the existence of the unknown, consider spirituality or religion to be a sign of gullibility. We cannot comment on each and every theory presented in spirituality and theology today, but we can assume that all of these beliefs are intended to grasp at that which is felt. We are not drawn to religion or spirituality initially due to it logically "adding up". This is impossible, as our reality is specifically designed to be penetrated only through faith, intuition and consciousness. We are drawn to these things because they resonate with our innermost truths, and whatever philosophy subjectively resonates more is the one we are most likely to frame our understanding of reality around. There is of course the problem of dogma, a result of harmless beliefs getting mixed in with the pesky human ego.

# EMPOWERMENT

Once the black man is aware of his own inner spirituality, he may then look to how he can use this gift to positively affect his life and the world around him. This first begins with self empowerment. Unfortunately black men have been systematically disempowered for centuries, influencing our subconscious minds. Your life, positive or negative, successful or impoverished is directly influenced by your mental attitude. To have a disempowered attitude is to allow the forces around you to be in control, not you.

Ultimately believing he is less, black men often find themselves struggling to attain greatness. The entirety of the black community has this systemic psychological problem which puts us at a fundamental disadvantage beginning from the earliest years of our lives. Masculinity is a force of movement and initiation of action. To essentially eradicate or suppress the capabilities of masculinity in the black community immobilizes us energetically. This manifests itself in the physical reality and we find on the whole, our community becomes one of vastly unrealized potential.

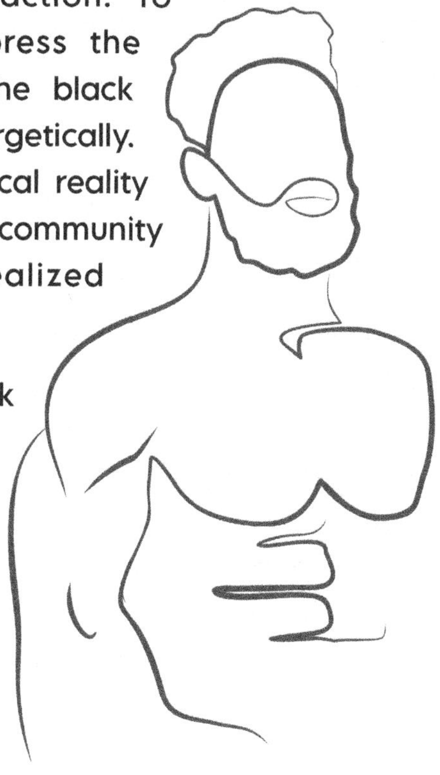

If we wish to mobilize the black community, the belief in our capabilities and commitment to action as a whole must be energized. This begins with a positive attitude towards our own empowerment. This is not to be confused with pride or supremacy, as this is usually a projection of in fact feeling less.

To be empowered is to understand you and you alone are 100% responsible and in control of your life and reality. It is extremely easy to believe that someone else reigns supreme above you and certain forces in this world will do everything they can to convince you of this. It is this belief alone which keeps the black man in his “place”.

If we wish to live the life of our dreams, we must first recognize our life is ours to mould and create. If we do not believe this, we cannot create any sort of life beyond what others choose for us. This is in accordance with the Law of Attraction or the principle of “like attracts like”.

Once black men recognize their own power, in truth much of the work is done automatically, as this paves the way towards the ambition. If you observe many celebrities, self-made millionaires and professional athletes, we see what separates them from the average person is the overwhelming sense of certainty that they will be successful. This goes beyond being motivated, and is the level of energetic intensity used for directing intention. The core of spirituality and many Eastern philosophies is the understanding that the mind and intention is everything.

The main difficulty with self empowerment with black men is undoing the brainwashing. The most effective way to do this is to be in a positive environment with those who are a reflection of where you desire to go. This will influence your own understanding of yourself and what you want to achieve. Positive black role male models are extremely fundamental in the developmental process of a black man, as what we observe outside will influence what we believe is possible within ourselves.

This process is daily and gradual. There is significance in the phrase "trust the process." Energy and intention can be put out and switched instantaneously, however the physical environment will often take some time to catch up. That is the nature of our dense reality. This will of course be difficult when there are huge amounts of temptation and information to lead black men astray.

# DISCIPLINE AND FOCUS

Discipline is very important for a healthy environment. In order for our dreams to be realized we need to commit to making our physical and mental environment an accommodating one. Manifesting desires is impossible if your environment is not compatible with what you want.

Of course there are many obstacles to the black man's success which have been inserted into his life or in the life of his forefathers which he will inherit.

Rather than demanding perhaps rightful compensation, it is our responsibility to ourselves and our children to create a physical and mental environment which accommodates success and prosperity ourselves. While it is certainly true some have a head start and others have more obstacles, all living beings are totally sovereign. What you start with can by no means be a barrier to where you desire to go, only a rest stop depending on perception. You may even

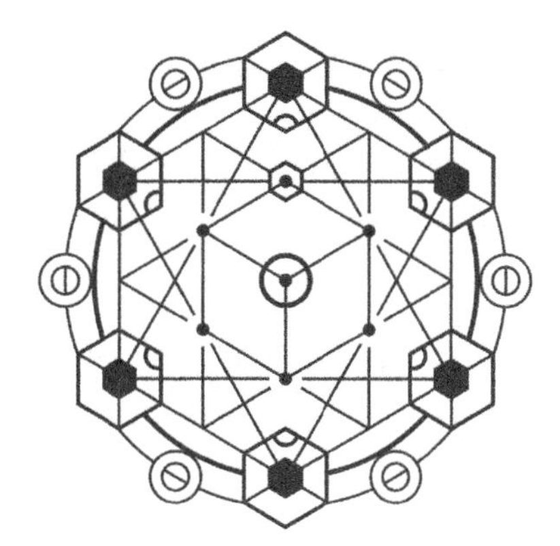

argue that having more obstacles puts you at a spiritual advantage, as you gain experience and strength which will serve yourself and others later.

Another important aspect of prosperity is focus. It is all well and good if your environment, companions and mental state are ready for prosperity, however we live in a world of distraction. A basic principle of the Law of Attraction is the importance of attention. Where you place your attention or energy is what the universe will prioritize in your reality. This world is overflowing with distractions, which serves as yet another weapon to use against the black man's (or anyones) freedom and prosperity.

We often have dreams which we commit to and believe in yet find the rate of progression to be extremely slow. How much attention do you put on this dream? This somewhat relates to energetic intensity, however it is not enough to simply believe in your success. To believe in your success and spend all of your time on other irrelevant things is to progress very slowly. The universe will prioritize your success in exact congruence with how much you prioritize it. This is why the system of working a 9-5 to survive is especially disempowering if stuck in positions which have nothing to do with our desires or ambitions. Attention is forced to be directed towards irrelevant things and we manifest less of what we want and more of what our employer wants.

There are also other examples. Many men suffer from the endless distraction which comes from obsessive sexual desire. If focused on drugs the same things applies. More drugs and more women are all we have to look forward to if we focus all of our attention towards drugs and women.

We do not suggest for one second that women are harmful for the black man's success, as that is simply untrue. Two people manifesting together always has double the power. I more refer to insatiable sexual desire which causes men to often not aim or strive towards anything aside from more sex. This is disempowering and takes energy and focus away from your movement towards your dreams. Simply put, all things are good and well in moderation.

The phrase "God is good" means that you receive exactly what you ask for, all the time. This "asking" is done through attention. What we understand as prayer is more an act of attempting to direct the attention.

THOUGHTS
BECOME
THINGS

# HOW BLACK MEN CAN USE THE LAW OF ATTRACTION

Choosing to embark on a journey of manifestation through the law of attraction is a form of self-care that every black man should embrace.

Where they may be barriers to entry that form as weapons against us we can choose to focus on our desires and breakthrough anything that stands in our way. With manifestation, we can take back our power.

## We can have it all.

From a life filled with luxury and the finer things to balance and harmony in all areas of our existence, now is our time to live our best lives! The law of attraction has swept through the black community and is educating us, from the young to the old more of us are cultivating a life that is filled with wealth, passion, and joy, all from this one simple secret.

Through generations of microaggressions and racism, we have been told that we are not destined to have joy in our lives. However, enough is enough. Regardless of the messages that we have faced from a society that has attempted to reject us, we still rise. Through manifestation, we are stepping into the best version of ourselves and changing the dynamics.

The law of attraction can open doors that were firmly held shut, turn around our circumstances and help us to create the lifestyle that we have always dreamt of.

Making time for spiritual practices and learning about who we are as individuals and as black men is essential. In a world where the color of our skin draws so much negativity toward us we have to protect ourselves physically, mentally, and spiritually.

It is through spirituality that we reclaim our greatness and deepen our connection to the metaphysical. Though our existence on this earth may prove to be challenging we can find faith and comfort through divination and manifestation. It is a source of healing that brings introspection and a heightened sense of awareness.

Black men are facing one of the most powerful eras in time that will shake the dynamics of society and shift our awareness. The world is slowly waking up to the greatness that we all hold inside, our spirituality is beckoning to us to recognize our greatness.

No more do we have to suffer when we have the answers to our prayers. Finally, the brothers are rising up in great numbers and discovering how incredible the law of attraction is. Take Will Smith, for example. He is a huge believer in the law of attraction and factors it as part of his success. If it can work for one black man it can work for all black men.

*"Our thoughts, our feelings, our dreams, our ideas are physical in the universe. That if we dream something, if we picture something, it adds a physical thrust towards the realization that we can put into the Universe."*

*Will Smith*

# THE POWER & HEALING

The law of attraction is working for us whether we are consciously using it or not. Once we start to utilize it and practice aligning ourselves with our desires we can shift our reality and transform our lives. By wanting the best for ourselves we are taking care of our needs.

Expect the best and go after your dreams. Part of self-care is realizing that you are meant to have an extraordinary life. It is your birthright to be abundant in whatever way feels good to you. Self-care is just as much mental and emotional as it is physical. The law of attraction can help us to look inside of ourselves and understand why we struggle to manifest our goals and what we can do about them.

If our aim is to attract certain desires then we need to believe that it is possible. For many of us, this is where we reach resistance. The blockages inside of us are called into question the moment that we start to use the law of attraction to our advantage. In the long run, we are pushed to challenge our negative beliefs and rewire ourselves to think more positively.

The healing and self-development that come with the use of the law of attraction are exactly what black men everywhere need. Manifesting can help us to think clearly about what we want, see ourselves in a more positive light and expect the best out of life.

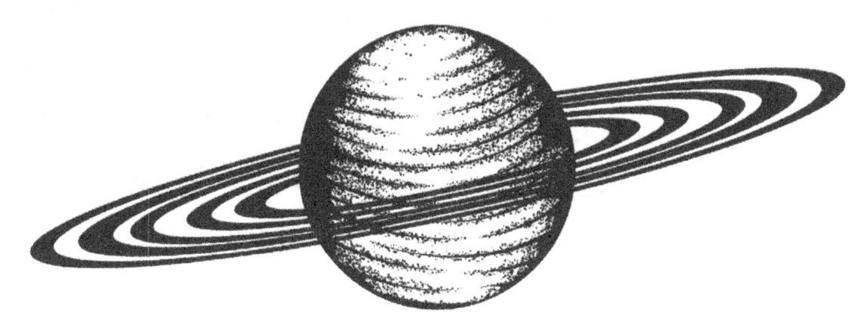

We can use the law of attraction to manifest the life of our dreams. No matter how big or small, we have the ability to take ourselves from the lowest points in our lives to the highest vibrational state. Prosperity and abundance are within our grasp.

We can go from rags to riches, lonely to loved up, and jobless to blessed. There is nothing that stands in our way, only the negative beliefs that have plagued our community. In this universe where everything is energy, we must learn how to shift our point of attraction and magnetize our desires.

Our thoughts and feelings are more powerful than we could ever know. By just changing the way that we see the world and ourselves we will become more empowered to go after our dreams and align ourselves with our goals.

Through the law of attraction, we can begin to heal from the psychological terror that we inherited from our ancestors. Once we choose a new direction and decide that we don't have to carry the weight and sadness that has held us down we can break free. Any mental barriers that have stood in our way will be vanquished.

All of the emotional trauma that we have held in our spirit will become no more once we focus on positive energy. Whether we want to be the first ones in our family to go to college, become a millionaire or have a successful career, we will do it.

Being black, we know the disadvantages that we have had to face however our past struggles are what is holding us back from prospering in the present and future. Whatever we believe about our finances is exactly what will take form. We have the power to completely change our lives and attract the fortune that we deserve.

Hold on to good thoughts, be thankful, and expect the best. The law of assumption teaches us to assume that we already have what we want and assume the feeling of having it. Taking this approach will release the flood of abundance into our lives and set the stage for more of it to come our way.

Many people have gone from dire financial situations to riches, all through the power of positive thinking and feelings. No situation is unchangeable, every circumstance that we face has the potential to shift entirely, regardless of what it is. We must elevate ourselves and make life work in our favor.

Too many of us resign ourselves to the current state of our reality, however, if we hold on to where we currently are we will never move forward.

Imagine yourself having purchased your dream house. Feeling your fingers wrap around the keys to your key home and feel yourself unlock the door. Visualize walking through your home and listen to the echo of your feet clicking against the floor. Imagine yourself holding the steering wheel of your dream car. See the lifestyle that you want, believe it to be true, and watch yourself flourish.

You can apply this method to any dream and desire. This is a powerful way that you can create the life you want and manifest the money you need.

*"That's how you do it, you've got to vision it first."*

*JAY Z*

# A MESSAGE TO ALL BLACK KINGS

Dear Brothers,

To every black man out there who is tired of the struggle and the strain, there no longer needs to be suffering. The law of attraction can take away sorrow and elevate us to new, powerful heights. There is so much that we have to offer and now it's time for the world to recognize the Kings within.

We want to see everyone win. We all deserve to win. Without a shadow of a doubt, we can all secure the prosperity that we want and live a life that is filled with wonder and possibilities. There are opportunities all around us, we just have to open our eyes to see them.

The secret has been in front of us all alone, it is inside of us waiting to break free. Now that the law of attraction has become more mainstream and information on how to use it is more accessible we should be taking advantage of it. This universal law is a gift that can propel us forward.

It is up to us to make the changes that we seek and take control of our reality. No one else can do that for us. We must be prepared to amend our beliefs, undo negative conditioning and attract the love and joy that awaits us.

We are meant to be happy - this is a fact of life. What holds us back from feeling like this is our observations of life and our reactions to it. We have the ability to choose more empowering thoughts and make our problems a thing of the past.

This manifestation journal was created with the intention to guide you to your greatest good. At this point in your spiritual evolution, you must surround yourself with resources and teachings that support you on your journey. You were made to flourish and fly, let this message be a confirmation of your greatness. So what should you do now?

Look inside yourself and see which areas need improving. Do you have a negative mindset that is preventing you from materializing your desires? Are your dreams struggling to manifest due to doubt, disbelief, and down days? The universe wants you to do the inner work and attend to your shadow self so that you can better yourself.

The law of attraction will work for you once you begin to work on yourself. It's only a moment of time until you break through the glass ceiling and blossom into the abundant being that you have always dreamt of being. Just trust the process and know that everything that you want is on its way to you. If you have asked and if you believe that you will receive.

Keep going and don't give up hope. No matter what challenges you face you can make it through to the other side and come out better and stronger than ever before. Your spirit guides are cheering you on as you take on this next chapter of your life, as are we.

Pursue your goals and soon enough you will see that it was all worth it.

On that note, we leave with these words of encouragement. Let our voice and words help you to tap into your spirituality and find the success that you have been looking for.

# LAW OF ATTRACTION

If you can take a moment to consider the raw power that the Law of Attraction holds, then it becomes very clear that you are the sole arbiter of your life. If you aren't happy with a certain part of your life, if you feel like you suffer or feel unfulfilled, you can use the Law of Attraction to change your life.

The Law of Attraction is a philosophical concept that poses the idea that positive thoughts will bring positive outcomes to you. The idea is primarily used in goal setting, turning negative beliefs into positive beliefs, and finding your overarching purpose in life. Several principles make up the basic foundation of the Law of Attraction.

## EVERYTHING IS A VIBRATION

Everything that manifests itself in your life is there because it matches the vibration from your thoughts.

Everything in the Universe is in a state of vibration. The word vibration has an unfortunate connotation that turns a lot of people off. For no reason indeed, because vibrations are based on physics. The idea that everything surrounding us, including us, is made up of vibrations, which means everything in the world is in a constant state of vibration. Even objects that appear to be stationary are in fact vibrating.

Think about the world as something you observe. You are engaging with all the energy that you come into contact with. You also create your own energy in your movements and even your thoughts and feelings. Our thoughts and feelings have a vibrational frequency. According to the Law of Attraction, like energy attracts like energy. So whether we're aware of it or not, the Universe merges with the vibrations we put out. That idea leads us to the following foundational idea.

## LIKE ATTRACTS LIKE

Things that are similar gravitate towards one another. That can be said for compatible couples, friend groups, event elements.

The idea is that your thoughts, attitudes, feelings, and all the other things that make up your vibrational energy will attract that which is similar. If you are putting out positive energy into the world, it will find you.

## NATURE HATES VACUUMS

Building on the idea that like attracts like is the idea that nature hates vacuums. The idea is that your mind and body can never be empty, and something always has to fill up space. If you don't actively fill your mind and body with positive thoughts, it will suck in the negative. Since the mind and the body always have to be full of something, it is better to actively fill it with positivity rather than be clouded by negativity.

*"You are what you think. So just think big, believe big, act big, work big, give big, forgive big, laugh big and love big"*

*Andrew Carnegie*

# BEING PRESENT

The idea that the present is already perfect is a central idea of the Law of Attraction practice.

While you might assume that because the Law of Attraction centers on looking towards the future, it would imply that there is something wrong with your life that should be changed. However, part of using the Law of Attraction focuses on the positive part of moving forward. Stay away from misery, unhappiness, or resentment towards your current situation; this clouds your energy negatively. You have to focus on the positive, which is bringing yourself good things, in order to move forward.

To use the Law of Attraction as a method of pursuing goals and desires, or even in bringing yourself closer to your ideal life, you have to carve out your own ideal reality. The idea sounds vague in theory but becomes firmer in practice. You are carving out your own reality to assist you in believing in something to bring it closer to yourself.

To do this, you have to find ways to incorporate the Law of Attraction into your daily life. This can be by,

- Practicing gratitude.
- Using visualization to visualize your goals.
- Learning how to identify negative thinking and turn it into positive thinking.
- Looking for the positive side of every situation.
- Using positive affirmations.

Because the Law of Attraction is the idea that we can attract into our lives what we choose to focus on, it is necessary that you incorporate the concepts mentioned above into your practice. That is because the Law of Attraction finds that all thoughts turn into energy that comes back to you. That means if you're not practicing gratitude or if you're not actively changing your negative thoughts, then those thoughts are manifesting negative energy towards you.

Similarly, the Law of Attraction places a huge emphasis on setting goals. You need to find something to focus your mind and energy on to channel the positive energy towards what you want to bring yourself.

*"I believe in the Law of Attraction and I believe that you can speak things into existence. And I believe that when you know where you're going and you know what you want, the Universe has a way of stepping aside for you."*

*Jonathan Dwight Jones*

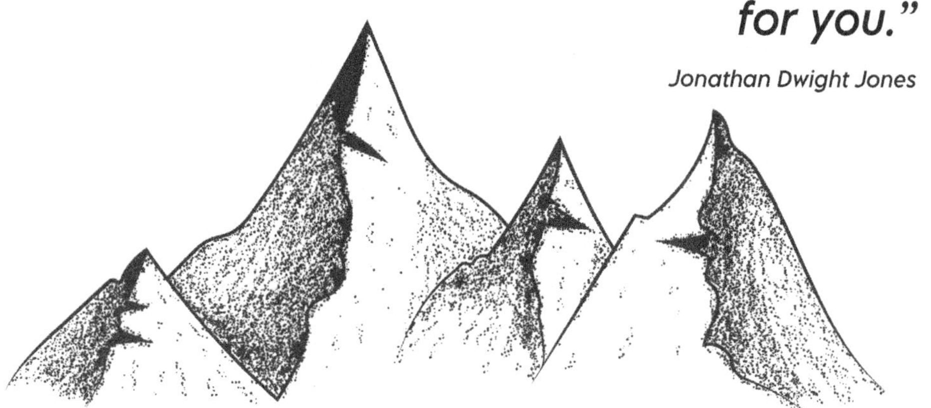

*"The Law of Attraction allows for infinite possibilities, infinite abundance, and infinite joy. It knows no order of difficulty, and it can change your life in every way."*

*Jack Canfield*

The law of attraction is a concept that is described through energy. What you put into the world, will come back to you. If you focus on positive thoughts, positive experiences will follow. Contrarily, if you spend time and energy on negative thoughts, negativity will ensue.

This is inherently about how you perceive and engage in the world. When you go through life optimistic, hopeful and excited, you are exuding that energy. The vibrations you send, will come back to you, and you will receive positive results in your life.

Every single thought is a vibration that is sent out into the universe. The law of attraction is not just about harnessing positive thoughts, so you land a promotion or a new job. It is about becoming fundamentally conscious of your thought process in everyday thought. We have control over what we believe, every minute of every day.

Tony Robbins is a world-renowned motivational speaker, author, and business coach. For years he has elevated the philosophy that there is power behind our thought process. He encourages people to think about the power within themselves, and to harness that power to produce positive results. In one example he discusses the power of certainty. He explains that when you are absolutely certain that something will change your life, you will do whatever it takes to make tha happen, because you are certain. If you do not believe that you can make a change, then you won't do it, because you are uncertain. And if you are unsure if you can make a change, or not, then you fall between those two camps of taking action, and not taking action. You simply don't know what to do. He shares that the difference in taking action and not doing so, is belief. He calls belief "the holy grail of belief," because it is so powerful. The difference in people is how they think, and how they view themselves in their mindset. Before you do something, you think about your potential, or lack thereof, and you analyze that level of potential. He describes a man who attempted to run a four-minute mile. He didn't think he could do it, because it simply hadn't been done for years and years. So, he didn't think he had the potential to run the four-minute mile. He thought, if someone else couldn't do it, why would I be able to? He attempted this feat anyway. He ran it and didn't make it under the four-minute time goal. So, he thought about what he could do differently. This time he focused on his mental state, to condition himself to get better. He already knew what to do physically to get in peak shape, but he hadn't done any mental training during his first time trial attempt. Through this mental exercise, he more closely examined his potential prior to taking action. He ended up running a four-minute mile, which was the exact result he wanted. Then after he received the result he wanted, this reinforced the notion that he was incredibly powerful, and he believed in himself. Following this event, not too long after that, over 37 people ran a four-minute mile. Why did this happen all of a sudden? It wasn't out of nowhere that an emergence of incredible athletes just got better physically. They believed that they could also run a four-minute mile. This example is so powerful, because of the cycle that takes place.

This example of believing in yourself was harnessed for running, but it can be applied to anything in your life.

The power of belief is essential to the Law of Attraction. You have to believe that you can make positive changes in your life. This is the crux of this story. People either take advantage of their potential or they don't. What happens when someone doesn't believe in themselves? If you believe that there's very little potential, how much action are you going to take? Not much. Then when you don't put much energy into action, then what will your results be? Not good. So, then you get poor results. What happens when you get poor results? You think negatively and tell yourself, "See I told you this wouldn't work." Then you feel as though you have even less potential. And you don't believe that you can do what you sought out to do. This is a dangerous path of self-destructive thinking. This can be applied to your career, your relationship, your friends, your family, and your hobbies. This negative self-talk will set you on a poisonous, downward spiral. Your thought process is a self-fulfilling prophecy. You have to combat it if you want to see changes in your life, in any way shape or form. Contrarily, if you get yourself in a state of certainty, then you tap into a lot of potential. Then you gain confidence to take big action, then when you get incredible results, you tell yourself, "See! I told you, you were awesome. I told you this would work out!" And that positive cycle continues to repeat itself. You believe that you can do whatever you want because you have that confidence and certainty that you can do it. You become so strong and gain so much momentum. Your energy is through the roof because you are so excited at what you just accomplished. If you think positively and believe in yourself you will carry that energy with you into all aspects of your life. This is the fundamental difference between people who are successful and people who struggle their way through life. The core difference in people is how you produce this belief and certainty. If you are uncertain and lack belief, you are facing a long road ahead. Only you have the power to change the trajectory of your life. It is possible to have the life you want.

This is what the Law of Attraction is all about. We have to believe we are capable of getting what we want in our lives. We have to be positive and have confidence in ourselves that we can do what we want, and get what we want, and live in a way that we only dream of for ourselves. The power of belief is essential in making changes in our lives.

So how do you become more confident and believe in yourself? Visualization is a powerful mental exercise to help achieve this mental state.

Tony Robbins shares another story about how he has worked with NBA players, and has trained them on the power of visualization. He shares that one of the problems that professional basketball players have is that despite all of their skill, they will choke on the free throw line in a game. This is a concept that can be confusing for a lot of people to understand. Why would a professional athlete, making millions of dollars every year, miss a shot when they are wide open, without anybody defending them? How is that possible that most NBA players don't make just about every shot when it's all they do? Well, the missing link is what is going on in their minds. There is a mental block, or a disconnect. We know they can shoot well when there isn't pressure, and that they know the fundamentals of how to stand, how to position themselves, and how to follow through. So why are they missing in games? One word: certainty. Tony tells us that these players are uncertain that they can make the shot. As simple as the shot is, they aren't sure if they can make the ball go into the hoop. To drive the point home about how important visualization is, he tells a story about a basketball team that is broken up into three groups. One group goes and practices free throws for six weeks. That's all they focus on. Just shooting as many shots as they can at the free throw line. The second group doesn't practice at all. They literally don't do anything. The third group works on their mental thought process. They don't touch a basketball, but they are coached to visualize themselves standing at the free throw line, making a shot every single time. They visualize shooting the ball, watching it leave their fingertips, arcing through the air, entering the hoop and swishing into the net. They never hold a basketball during this practice. They just visualize themselves shooting with the ball going into the hoop, and that they are bringing their team extra points.

At the end of the six weeks, all three groups meet to shoot free throws and see what team performs the best. Unsurprisingly, the second team that did nothing, did not perform well. The team that practiced shooting free throws every day remained the same. They didn't get better or worse. In the end, it was the third group that mentally trained, who performed the best. Through the power of visualization and mental conditioning, they trained their brains to believe that they would make every shot. This story is incredibly powerful, because it shows just how much power our brains have, and how much we can learn from certainty and believing in ourselves. If NBA players who make millions are employing this thought process, then it can work for the rest of us.

*"I can accept failure, everyone fails at something. But I can't accept not trying."*

*Michael Jordan*

WHAT

YOU FEEL

YOU WILL

ATTRACT

# MANIFESTATION

Manifestation is a similar idea to the Law of Attraction in fact you will often hear them used interchangeably. However, while the Law of Attraction is the idea that you have to use the positive power of your thoughts to bring yourself positive experiences and things. Manifestation is based on the same idea but speaks directly to what you need to do to achieve it.

Essentially, manifestation and the Law of Attraction go hand-in-hand. Manifestation is putting your intention towards something that you hope will happen, then watching it happen in real life.

Manifestation techniques are the things you do, such as daily rituals or practices, which help you utilize the Law of Attraction to achieve your goals. In this journal more of these techniques will be explained, but they may include:

- Visualization.
- Using vision boards.
- Cutting out self-limiting beliefs or thoughts.
- Gratitude journaling.
- Affirmations.

Manifestation techniques are the powerful tools you use to work within the Law of Attraction, they ensure that you can bring yourself the positive things you want that make up your dreams and desires. You will notice that the list above, includes some vague sounding things, like affirmations and visualization, but also, some tangible and normal things that plenty of people use every day. Journaling or using vision boards is a popular manifestation technique, and one that doesn't require a great deal of spiritual practice. Many people use vision boards or use journals to record their gratitude, goals or dreams, and may not even recognize that they are manifesting. That is because manifesting and using the Law of Attraction can be something you pursue either with or without intention. Your results will be more powerful if you conduct actions with intention, like in pursuing anything.

Everything happening in your life is a reflection of what is happening inside of you. Your world is a reflection of you. Whatever you focus on will take shape and manifest into your daily life. It's so important to know exactly how to use your manifesting power.

Putting your dreams and goals on paper can help you to manifest your desire. When you feel lost or unsure about your manifesting process, or even get frustrated, check back on your goals and insights to find guidance. Your manifesting journal is an ongoing process.

Throughout the rest of this journal, we're going to dive deeper into the Law of Attraction and Manifestation. You will receive a tangible step-by-step guide that explains specific methods and techniques you can use to approach the Law of Attraction.

Overall, this journal is going to help you unpack and understand these techniques and methods and what might seem daunting will be much less so by the end of this journal. The goal here is to provide you with a firm set of options when following the Law of Attraction and using manifestation.

# HOW TO USE THE LAW OF ATTRACTION AND MANIFESTATION

## THINK ABOUT IT FIRST

One of the most important things to do before you get started manifesting and using the Law of Attraction is to take a step back and take stock of what you want to get out of the process. You need to take your time to assess yourself and make sure that you want what you want. Manifestation is no joking matter, and you need to make sure that what you're trying to bring into your life is what you want in your life.

You also need to be specific as you possibly can in your desires, affirmations, and manifestations. That is because it's very difficult to bring a broad idea closer to yourself. You shouldn't pick things like happiness. That is too vague. You have to zone in on the things that will provide you happiness, like love or wealth. If at all possible, try to go beyond those things, which are still slightly vague in nature. When you are doing that work, you should stick with things that bring you passion and excitement. If the idea of wealth is very exciting and provides you with happiness, then that would be something worth manifesting. However, if you just want to find love because it feels like the right thing to do, then you might need to step back further and re-evaluate what you want to gain from the process.

# DEVELOP A CLEAR MIND

There is a good reason that so many people who use the Law of Attraction and manifestation are avid meditators. It is because the mind needs to be cleared before you can start on your journey of seeking to fulfill your dreams.

It is necessary to check whether you find all of your beliefs and thoughts necessary when bringing forth new desires and dreams. That is especially true when you consider that the Law of Attraction's entire point is to cleanse your mind of negative thoughts. You need to take a brief inventory of your thoughts, feelings, and ideas about the world. Think about whether they are positive. Think about whether they serve you in your long-term goals. If they don't fit or don't make you feel good, then they must be released.

Additionally, any of your own fears and anxieties are limiting and create problems when you manifest. You have to remove the fear and anxiety from your thoughts. They hold you back and should be treated as illusions. They are inhibiting your success, which you must recognize in order to pursue your goals.

After clearing your mind, which you can consider as a type of spring cleaning of the mind, you should feel more positive. You should feel less anxious and guilty. If you can fill your thoughts with positivity it smooths the road ahead and makes it an easier path forward.

*"The mind has a powerful way of attracting things that are in harmony with it, good and bad."*

*Idowu Koyenikan*

# TRUST

You also need to develop a level of trust in the process. Many life coaches who coach in the Law of Attraction and manifestation will tell you that you need to trust the process blindly and surrender yourself to the law. That is absolutely true.

Your success in using these methods and techniques rests on your ability to believe in yourself and in the Law of Attraction. That is always difficult for beginners to achieve who have the seeds of doubt planted firmly in the back of their minds. However, it's helpful to remind yourself that the Law of Attraction and any manifestation technique is a direct product of your own ability to make it happen. If you can foster even a tiny seed of belief in yourself, then it will make it a whole lot easier to work with. Also, remember that the Law of Attraction is based on very simple beliefs and principles. You need to have the belief that your wishes will be fulfilled and that they deserve to be fulfilled.

# USING VISUALIZATION

There are a few different methods of visualization, and it can be interpreted across a few methods of conduct. The basic definition of visualization is that it is a mental process of forming visual-based images or interpreting visual-based ideas and then putting them into visible form. That sounds extremely vague and confusing. So, let's simplify it.

Visualization is basically mentally picturing and thinking about the things you want to come into your life or the things you wish were already in your life. Visualization is usually done during mindfulness practices like meditation. You would want to sit or lay down in a quiet place or any place in which you practice mindfulness and meditation and pair your visualization with it. You can also do visualizations while you're going to sleep, on the bus or train to work, or enjoying your morning coffee. It's an adaptable technique that can be paired with relaxing activities. You can take a bath and do visualizations or do them while you're doing light exercise. Find out what works best for you and put it into place.

If you haven't done visualization before, you may be a skeptic. However, you can think about visualization as a way you train your mind and prepare for experiencing something you want. That is extremely helpful because if you picture something coming into your life, the more likely it begins to seem that it will.

Visualization also creates a motivational mindset. It's sort of like a mental vision board, which we'll discuss later on. If you keep visualizing something, you are actively creating a mindset that wants to pursue it. You visualize the thing over and over again and begin to believe that it could enter your life, it then either becomes drawn to you, or you come upon opportunities that may make that thing happen.

Visualization additionally helps you identify what you really want. That is helpful for intention setting, which is a key element of many manifestation practices.

*"I always visualize good things. I always visualize victory, success, abundance. I visualized it all, and it's all happening."*

*Conor McGregor*

# REMINDER BEFORE WE START

The Law of Attraction is a universal and a very powerful law. It reacts to the words you say, your thoughts and the emotions you experience. It makes endless abundance, infinite possibilities, infinite joy, and happiness possible.

Making a lifestyle change is difficult, especially when you want to alter several things at once. The tough part is committing and following through after you've decided to make a change. Making the changes you desire requires time and dedication, but you can do it. Just keep in mind that no one is flawless. It's inevitable that you'll make mistakes every now and again. Be kind to yourself. Maintain your focus on the fact that this is not a contest.

Relax and work at your own pace. Manifestation is similar to a mental workout. Just as with physical exercise, you may need to try a few different things until you find what works best for you. The more you learn about what happens when you use the Law of Attraction, the better. If you truly want to succeed, you must approach the Law of Attraction with long-term goals in mind. The adjustments you're implementing aren't intended to be transient. They are designed to be a component of a new way of living that you adopt in order to manifest your dream life.

You are constantly in the process of creating something new. The Law of Attraction, like gravity, is always in motion. It is always drawing things that are vibrationally aligned with your ideas and feelings. Have faith in the Law of Attraction. Believe in its effectiveness. Have trust in your ability to make it happen for you. Believe in your ability to succeed. Always remember:

# YOU ARE THE CREATOR OF YOUR OWN REALITY

# HERE ARE THE STEPS TO MANIFEST YOUR DREAM LIFE

- GET CLEAR ON WHAT YOU WANT.
- VISUALIZE YOUR DESIRE OR DREAM LIFE.
- FEEL THE ENERGY OF YOUR DESIRE.
- USE AFFIRMATIONS TO REPLACE LIMITING BELIEFS.
- HAVE FAITH.
- KEEP YOUR VIBRATION HIGH.
- MATCH THE FREQUENCY OF THE REALITY YOU WANT.
- ALWAYS TRUST YOUR INTUITION.
- RELEASE CONTROL.
- BE PURPOSEFUL WITH YOUR THOUGHTS AND BELIEFS.
- KEEP IN MIND THAT REPETITION AND INTENTION IS KEY.
- CAREFULLY WATCH YOUR THOUGHTS - YOU ARE WHAT YOU THINK.
- ALIGN ACTIONS WITH YOUR GOALS .
- TAKE INSPIRED ACTION - HELP THE UNIVERSE MAKE IT HAPPEN.
- LET GO OF ANY RESISTANCE AND LIMITING BELIEFS.
- TRUST THE PROCESS.

# ANSWER THE PROMPTS BELOW

In order to attract abundance, wealth, success and happiness, you must first decide what you want. Questions have power. And by addressing deep questions you will get profound answers. Start by taking a few minutes to clear your mind, and get into a relaxed state. Close your eyes and take 5 deep breaths. Anything you feel an impulse to write, allow it.

Where do I see myself in one year?

..........................................................................................................................

Where do I see myself in five years?

..........................................................................................................................

Where do I see myself in ten years?

..........................................................................................................................

What is currently keeping me from living my dream life? One word:

..........................................................................................................................

What can I do to change this?

..........................................................................................................................

..........................................................................................................................

..........................................................................................................................

Is the life that I am living the life I want to be living?

..........................................................................................................................

..........................................................................................................................

..........................................................................................................................

Am I a fulfilled person?

..........................................................................................................................

..........................................................................................................................

..........................................................................................................................

What parts of my life don't reflect who I am?

..........................................................................................................................

..........................................................................................................................

If I could live anywhere in the world, where would I live and why?

........................................................................................................

How satisfied am I with my life?

........................................................................................................

........................................................................................................

........................................................................................................

........................................................................................................

........................................................................................................

........................................................................................................

What I desire the most in my life is?

........................................................................................................

........................................................................................................

........................................................................................................

........................................................................................................

What would I do if I knew I couldn't fail?

........................................................................................................

........................................................................................................

........................................................................................................

What, and who, deserves my attention?

........................................................................................................

........................................................................................................

........................................................................................................

Do the people I surround myself with add any value to my life?

........................................................................................................

........................................................................................................

........................................................................................................

........................................................................................................

........................................................................................................

Am I holding onto something I need to let go of? What do I need to let go of to move to that next level in life?

........................................................................................................

........................................................................................................

........................................................................................................

What would I want to experience in life if money was not an issue?

How do I want to grow?

How does success look like to me?

Write down the reasons why you believe you are not successful yet. What would you do differently if you knew nobody would judge you? What is holding you back? What limiting beliefs are holding you back?

Write down more empowering and supportive beliefs you want to be a part of your new life story.

# I RELEASE...

What are you holding onto right now that no longer serves you? Let go of what holds you back, so you can attract more of what you really want.

# SELF-DISCOVERY

What are the things you need to improve and work on?

Is everything in your life going too fast, too slow, or just right?

Where are you living right now - in the past, future, or present?

Are you made to work for others or yourself?

In what areas of your life are you settling?

What makes you happy and relaxed?

What makes you feel motivated, inspired, and excited?

Have you been holding yourself back? How can you change that?

What do you want to be able to say about your life when you're 70?

How would you like to be remembered?

# SELF-ASSESSMENT

In the middle circle write your name. Then answer the prompts to describe yourself. If you ask yourself the following questions, you'll raise your self-awareness and start making better decisions. Self-awareness is a key component of success.

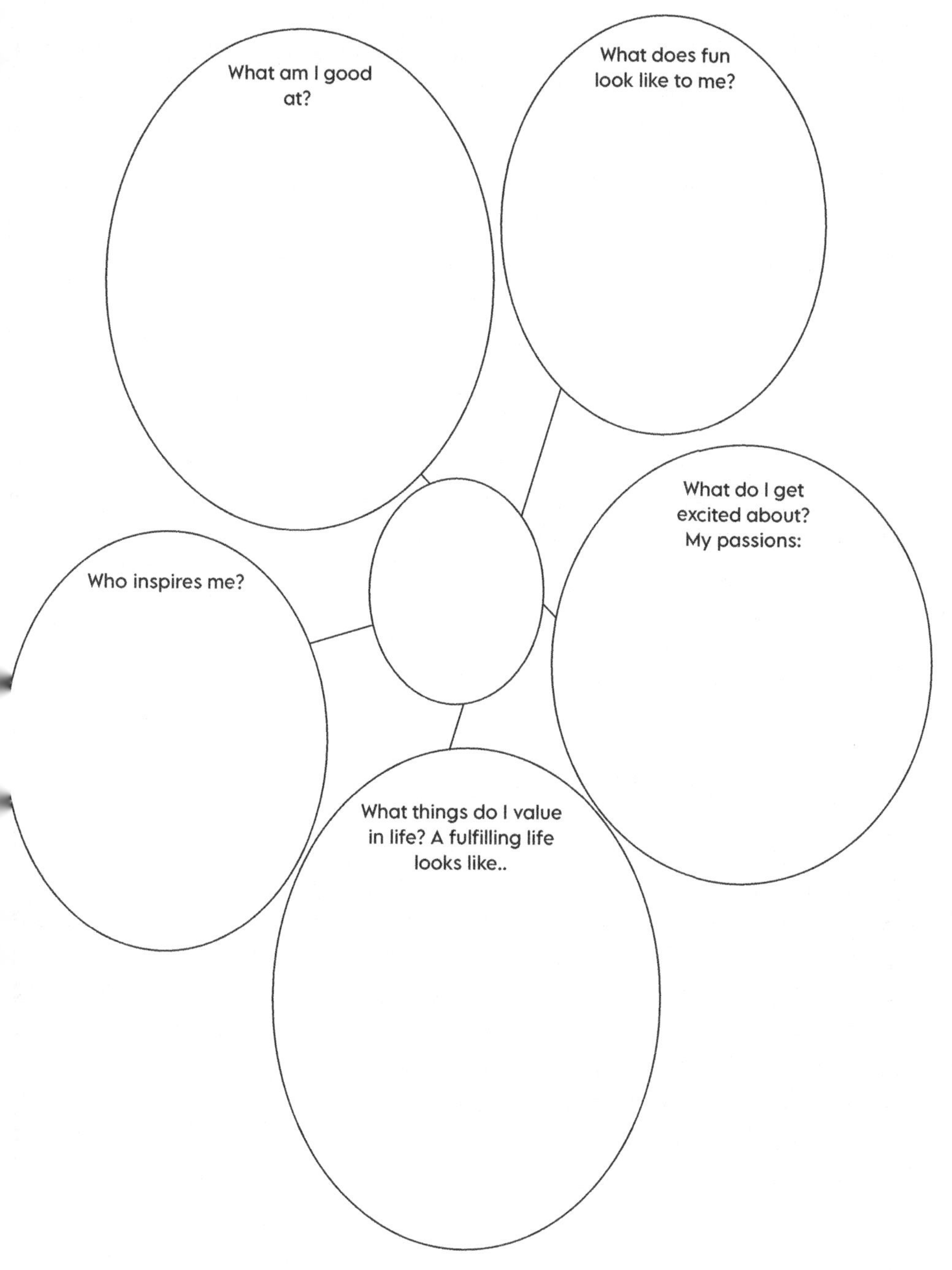

# LIFE CHANGES

Write down your vision of where you want to go in each level of your life and write down how you will achieve your goals. These questions will help you paint a clearer picture of what you want to do with your life.

First consider the areas that most need renewed attention or that have been unintentionally neglected.

## WHERE AM I RIGHT NOW?

Which parts of your life are strong and vibrant? Which areas are often neglected?

## WHERE DO I WANT TO BE?

To truly be able to pursue the goal of having everything you want in life, you need to have an incredibly vivid and detailed vision for what you want in all aspects of your life, including: HEALTH, SPIRITUALITY, CAREER, RELATIONSHIPS, FAMILY, PERSONAL DEVELOPMENT, FINANCES. Once you begin to have a clear vision for what you want in each of these categories, then you can truly start thinking about how to achieve everything you want in life.

## HOW CAN I GET THERE?

Think about where do you want to be in each of those categories listed in #2 and then break them down into more manageable steps. It is never too late to become the person you have always hoped you could be. We often forget that we are not bound by our past. We don't have to be who we were a year ago. We have to believe that we are never too old, never too jaded, and never too broken to take our first steps towards change. We wake up every single day with the ability to start fresh - it is never too late to take advantage of that! It's never too late to do what you're passionate about and what you truly desire!

| | WHERE AM I NOW? | WHERE DO I WANT TO BE? | HOW CAN I GET THERE? |
|---|---|---|---|
| HEALTH | | | |
| SPIRITUAL | | | |
| CAREER | | | |
| RELATIONSHIP | | | |
| FAMILY | | | |
| FINANCES | | | |
| PERSONAL DEVELOPMENT | | | |

# MISSION STATEMENT

A mission statement defines your purpose in life, it summarizes your values and goals. In essence, it's a statement about who you are and how you will live your life.

We all have goals (or at least we think we do) we are trying to achieve in life. But bonding them together, polishing and organizing them, and then using them to formulate a strong mission statement can make a lot of difference in your life journey.

A mission statement will help you stay focused and inspire you to put in more effort towards achieving your goals. Your mission statement will always be the driving force that continues to push you and ensure you don't take your eyes off your life's purpose.

We know the importance of visualization when it comes to the law of attraction and manifesting your heart desires. Creating a mission statement can help you envision the future and ensure it's always in your line of view. Remember you are more likely to achieve anything you constantly have your sight on. Another reason to keep a mission statement is that it can help you align your behaviors. The outcome you are trying to achieve requires small, simple, and consistent actions that keep moving you towards that goal. These small actions add up over time to gradually make your dreams a reality.

Your mission statement should contain a summary of specific actions you will be taking towards achieving your goals and purpose in life.

# MY MISSION STATEMENT

# SETTING GOALS

This is the time for you to attract the lifestyle you want. If change is calling your name, answer! Don't get stuck in a rut, make a plan for how you're going to switch things up and reroute the direction of your life. Use our tips to guide you into making effective goals. They'll push you to become the best version of yourself and build a new and improved life for yourself.

*"Whatever you are imagining, you are attracting into your life."*

## DON'T BE 'REALISTIC'

How many times have you had a dream only to be told that you need to be practical, sensible, and rational? Though it's often said out of love, this so-called advice can hold you back from realizing your potential. The fact of the matter is anything is possible with the law of attraction so trying to be 'realistic' could keep you from living your best life.

If you believe in yourself then you will achieve your goals and bring your dreams to life. The only limitations that exist are the ones that you have formulated in your mind. Take control! Now is the perfect moment to break through your blockages and prove to the world that you can be, do and have everything that you want.

## BE SPECIFIC

When you're attempting to manifest you need to be specific about what you want. The universe likes clarity, the more detailed you are about your goals the more accurate your manifestations will become. Take money for example. Some people make the mistake of asking for more of it rather than specifying how much they want.

Setting your intention to manifest more money could mean that you receive less than what would make you happy. After all, attracting a dollar is technically manifesting more money, is it not? If you want to be successful in your life you need to know what you want and go after it!

Start by looking at your current circumstances and make a list of things that you want to change. It can include every area of your life including your health and wellness, career, friendships, and love. Get a clear picture of what you want and you can begin the process of manifesting your desires.

*"Thoughts become things."*

## HAVE FUN

One of the most important tips that you should take into consideration is to enjoy the process. As black men, we have so much to bear and deal with on a daily basis. Our spiritual practices and manifestation rituals should take away some of that strain, not add to it! When you're determining what you want make sure that it brings you joy and have fun with the attraction process.

If something feels forced or unnatural you need to reevaluate whether or not it is right for you. Don't be afraid to question your goals if they don't bring you happiness. By removing obstacles to your success you will find the abundance that you deserve.

# MY GOALS

Having goals is like having a map. You know where you are heading, and this gives you motivation.

| SET GOALS IN ALL AREAS OF YOUR LIFE |
|---|
| 1. |
| 2. |
| 3. |
| 4. |
| 5. |
| 6. |
| 7. |
| 8. |
| 9. |
| 10. |

## CHOOSE AND FOCUS ON TOP 5 GOALS FROM YOU LIST AND ASK YOURSELF - WHY ARE THESE GOALS IMPORTANT TO ME?

| GOAL | WHY? |
| --- | --- |
| 1. | |
| 2. | |
| 3. | |
| 4. | |
| 5. | |

## REWARD YOURSELF FOR ACHIEVING YOUR GOALS

| ACHIEVED | REWARD |
| --- | --- |
| 1. | |
| 2. | |
| 3. | |
| 4. | |
| 5. | |

# GOAL SETTING

Ask yourself - how will I make it happen?
Start taking action steps to achieve your goals.

| MY GOAL | WHAT ARE MOST IMPORTANT STEPS TO MAKE IT HAPPEN? |
| --- | --- |
| | 1.<br>2.<br>3.<br>4.<br>5. |
| | 1.<br>2.<br>3.<br>4.<br>5. |
| | 1.<br>2.<br>3.<br>4.<br>5. |
| | 1.<br>2.<br>3.<br>4.<br>5. |
| | 1.<br>2.<br>3.<br>4.<br>5. |

# BUCKET LIST

On the left side write down all the things you want to *EXPERIENCE*. On the right side write down all the things you want to *ACHIEVE*.

| EXPERIENCES | ACHIEVEMENTS |
| --- | --- |
| | |

# READ OUT LOUD

I AM THE CREATOR OF MY REALITY.

I AM THE ARCHITECT OF MY LIFE.

I AM FREE OF LIMITING BELIEFS.

I AM ATTRACTING ENDLESS
ABUNDANCE INTO MY LIFE.

# CREATE A VISION BOARD

There's something wonderful about putting your big ideas, desires, dreams and goals down on paper. Investing time and work in creating a vision board can not only help you get clear on what you want to accomplish in your life, but it will also help your dreams come true. A vision board brings the dream to life in your imagination, allowing you to feel it is possible.

A vision board is a tangible depiction of the goals you want to attain. Having a visual reminder will assist you in remaining focused. A vision board also fosters an emotional connection that encourages you. It's always amazing to go back and look at an old vision board and discover how many dreams have come true! Consider the following:

- What are your most important dreams and goals?
- What will each aspect of your life look like once you've realized your dream?
- Consider your dreams in the following areas: relationships, work, finances, house, travel, personal development, and health. Your vision board should be focused on how you want to feel rather than just what you desire.
- You may also split your vision board into categories; having your vision board separated into particular categories might help you be clear on how you want your life to develop (categories can include: relationships and family, finances, career or business, health and fitness, travel, education and hobbies, spirituality and material possessions).

  Put anything that inspires and drives you on your vision board.

  Every day, take a few moments to reflect on your vision board. At least once a day, pause and evaluate the visuals, statements, and goals.

# MY VISION BOARD

# MY VISION BOARD

# MIND MAP

Mind maps are effective visual representations that help you organize your ideas. A finished mind map provides you with a higher-level view of your concepts in general. Simply jotting down all of your goals in one spot will most likely provide you with valuable insight into your life.

Begin by free-writing any ideas, feelings, or observations you have concerning your health, money, family, spirituality, relationships, vacation plans, work aspirations, and personal development objectives.

To generate ideas, consider the following:

*-What is most significant to me about this part of my life, and why?*

*-What is the one thing I would alter if I had the chance?*

*-How would success ideally seem to me?*

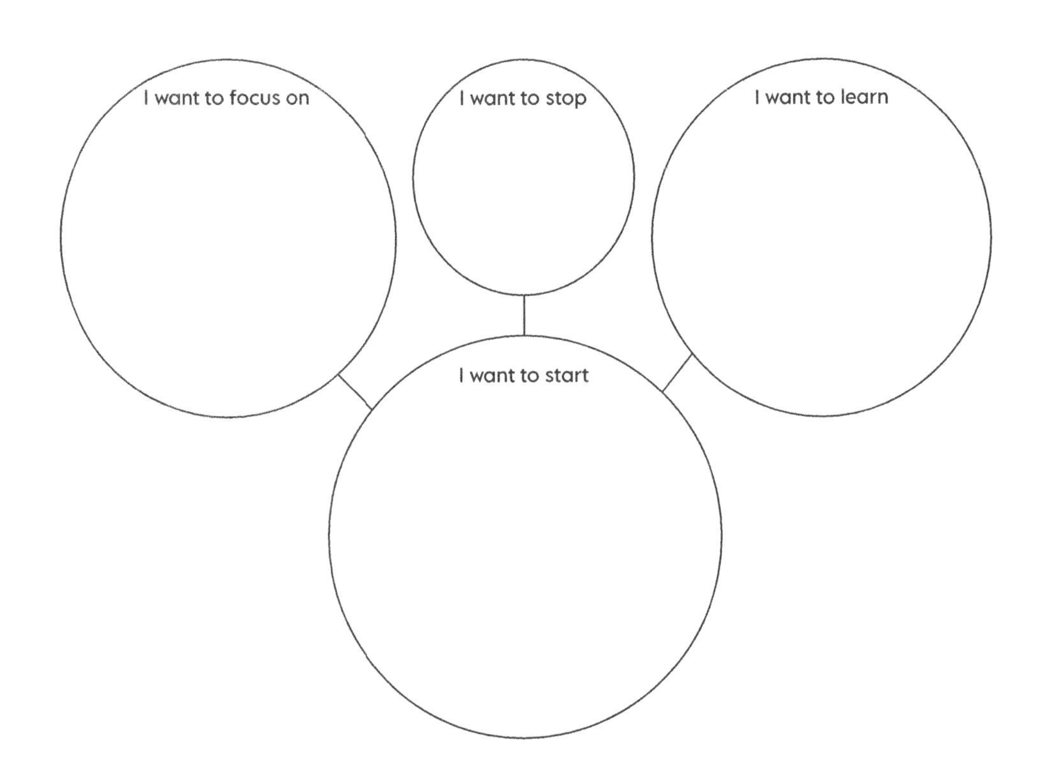

# MIND MAP

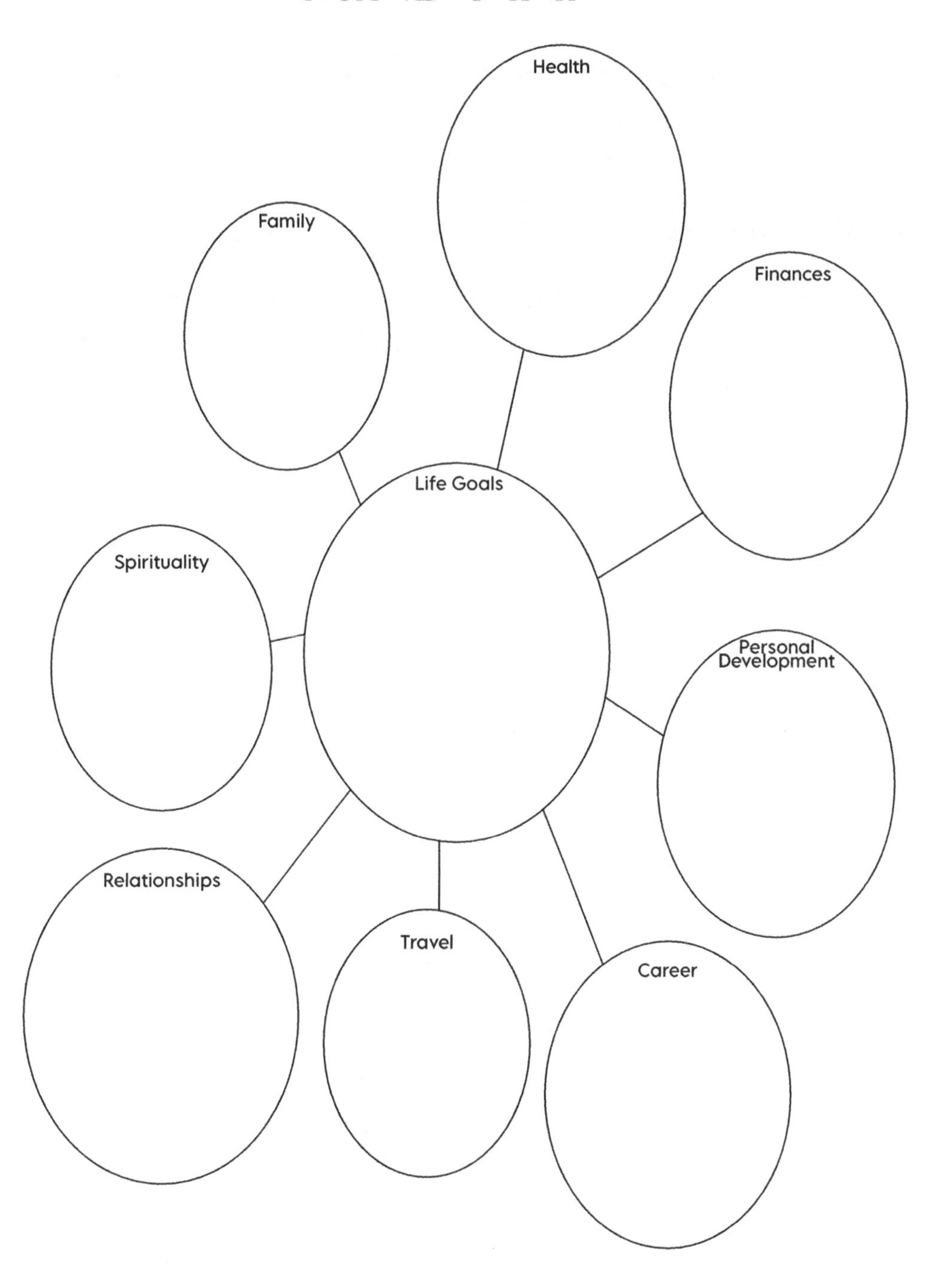


*"Whatever you hold in your mind on a consistent basis is exactly what you will experience in your life."*

*Tony Robbins*

# FEAR SETTING

You are trapped by fear, but it does not have to own you. Fear is a natural emotion that we all encounter from time to time. Because you are human, you are afraid.

Tim Ferriss inspired the Fear Setting practice.

Fear setting is a technique for visualizing all of the awful things that may happen to you in order to reduce your fear of taking action.

How many times have you been stopped by fear of what could happen rather than acting on something you truly wanted to do?

Consider Fear Setting to be the polar opposite of Goal Setting. Make a checklist of what you are frightened to do and what you are worried will happen instead of a list of what you want to do.

*"The brave man is not he who does not feel afraid, but he who conquers that fear."*

*Nelson Mandela*

| DEFINE<br>What are the worst things that could happen? | PREVENT<br>How do I prevent each from happening? | REPAIR<br>If the worst happens, how can I fix it? | BENEFITS<br>Possible benefits if successful | COSTS<br>If I avoid doing this thing what might I miss out on? |
| --- | --- | --- | --- | --- |
| | | | | |
| | | | | |
| | | | | |

I DREAM.
I BELIEVE.
I RECEIVE.

# MANIFESTING MONEY

Have you ever looked at your bank account and felt frustrated? You work hard, you save up and somehow it still doesn't seem to be enough. Money is one of the most talked-about topics particularly when the law of attraction comes into play. If people can manifest love, happiness and good health with this universal law then surely money is possible, right?

The answer is absolutely! The law of attraction is the concept of 'like entering into like'. It states that everything in the universe is made of energy. Your thoughts and feelings attract specific people, life events and outcomes which match that energetic vibration. This also includes the state of your finances. So how can you use the law of attraction and what methods can you implement to manifest the wealth and abundance that you want? Read on to find out everything that you need to know.

# THE KEY STEPS TO MANIFESTING MONEY WITH THE LAW OF ATTRACTION

If you want to boost your bank balance and create the lifestyle that you have always wanted you have to understand how the law of attraction works. Once you know the steps to manifesting the money you want you will transform your life in ways that you have never known. You need to familiarize yourself with the 'how to' before you start to take action so you can ensure your success.

These steps are simple, easy and straightforward to implement. With a little practice, you can go from broke to wealthy in no time at all. The law of attraction has been used by some of the biggest names such as Oprah, Will Smith and Jim Carrey. Each one has used these exact principles to bring them immense amounts of money and fame. If they can do it then so can you.

## SET YOUR INTENTION

If you don't know what you want, how can you ask for it? The process of conscious manifestation is the magic formula that will make your dreams come true. In the story Aladdin, the genie asks him to make three wishes. If Aladdin did not set his intention and state exactly what he wants he wouldn't have received what he wanted.

The same principle applies to you when you are seeking to manifest money. You have to know exactly what you want and communicate that to the universe. Many people who want to improve their finances will try to manifest 'more money', but what does that mean? More money could be anything from $5 to $1,000,000 so you have to be specific.

The universe takes your intentions at face value so detail is the key to ensuring that your manifestations come true. To help you clarify what you want, pick a specific amount of money and use that as your focus. The law of attraction manifests what your energy is aligned to and so you need to choose what vibration you want to connect with.

To further set your intention, write out a list of everything that you plan on spending your money on. Think about how that money could help you and focus on the benefits that it holds. Let this money become your deepest desire and that amount will surely be available to you.

## BELIEVE

Your thoughts, mindset and beliefs are what influences your experiences. Your subconscious mind is where these attributes are held which creates your reality. You have to believe with all of your heart, mind and soul that it is possible for you to have the money that you want. You are a creative being with the power to attract all of the money you could ever dream of. You need to trust in your ability and feel the universal power that flows through your veins. Nothing is too much for you to manifest.

All of your thoughts have power and so if your words are saying 'I have manifested $10,000' but your mind is thinking 'that's not possible' then you will struggle to attract the money that you want. If you know that something is possible then you remove any resistance that you may have and it can easily become part of your experience.

Take ordering from a restaurant, for example. When you sit down at your table and the waiter takes your order you don't keep reordering your meal because you are unsure that it will come. You wouldn't doubt yourself because you feel as though the restaurant won't give you your food. No. You know that as soon as you make your intention clear the information for your order will be relayed to the kitchen and the chef will start making your food.

As soon as you make your intention clear the universe sets the wheels in motion. As long as your vibration matches what you want to manifest you can be sure that it will come to you.

Believing in your power sustains your manifestation, the moment that you start to question whether or not it is possible you prevent it from taking form. Now is the time to relax and believe.

## RECEIVE

This is the last stage in the manifestation process and the part where you will reach your financial goals. Imagine that you receive everything that you have been asking for. All the money that you wanted to attract has flowed into your life. Suddenly, you can now book the perfect vacation, buy that dream house and treat your loved ones. How would you feel? Excited!

To receive you need to feel as though it has already happened and feel the emotions of having it. Become the very thing that you have been asking for and celebrate your win! When you get the amount of money that you want you will feel elated and overjoyed so therefore that is exactly what you should be feeling. Some people make the mistake of sinking into a feeling of lack. If their manifestation is taking too long they start to question the validity of the law of attraction and start wondering 'WHERE IS MY MONEY?!'. However long it takes to manifest it will work in divine timing. The moment that you start to focus on not having what you have asked for it will cease to be. When you plant a seed in the ground you don't keep digging it up to check if it's growing. You feel good that it is on its way to you and you shower it with life-affirming water, or in your case, you continue to think positive thoughts. Be open to receiving and expect the money that you want to come to you. Don't focus on the how, just let it be and go with the flow.

“

TODAY IS YOUR OPPORTUNITY TO BUILD THE TOMORROW YOU WANT.

# CHANGING YOUR LIMITING BELIEFS ABOUT MONEY

So you now know the steps to manifesting money. The belief aspect of this theory is one of the most important parts of mastering the law of attraction for wealth. It can be the difference between staying where you are or progressing and achieving extraordinary levels of prosperity.

Your belief system is the foundation for your life. It outlines everything that you are attracting into your world. From how much money you have made in your career to those moments when you always seem to attract money at certain times, it is all down to the subconscious beliefs that you hold in your mind.

Life mastery through the law of attraction involves empowering yourself and feeding your mind with positive new beliefs. If you feel as though you are not meant to be rich then according to the law that will be your reality. If you question whether or not you deserve to be financially free you will always be kept in a position of 'just getting by'. However, if you know, trust and believe that abundance is your birthright then you will never have to worry about money again.

Shifting your beliefs is one of the best things that you can do for your self-development and your finances. When you work through your limiting beliefs it will trigger remarkable changes in your life and will affect the relationship that you have with money. When you work on yourself then the universe will work in your favor. If you want to change your money mindset then first you have to...

## IDENTIFY YOUR LIMITING BELIEFS

Life isn't happening to you, it is being shaped by the many thoughts and beliefs that you express on a daily basis. We live our lives on autopilot and naturally fall into a rhythm that helps us to move from one day to the next. When you start to become aware of your beliefs and change them you effectively grab the wheel and control the direction that your life is going in. To shift your beliefs you need to work out what they are. This takes a certain amount of honesty and openness where you are able to work through the thoughts that you have toward money.

To help you make sense of what you are feeling, write out how you feel about your job, salary, the money you have in your bank account, what you heard about money growing up and any dismissive comments that anyone has made toward you about achieving your dreams. As hard as it may be, you will soon feel good about this process as it will show you what you need to work on. You may identify that the reason you are always in debt is that a parent constantly complained about owing money while you were growing up. If you have struggled with making a business work you may be holding onto negative comments made about you becoming an entrepreneur. Whatever negative belief that you write out is exactly what you need to change. These are the beliefs that are holding you back from greatness and now is the moment that you change them forever

## PIVOT YOUR BELIEFS

Just as easily as you acquired these beliefs you can change them. Your mind is like a sponge that absorbs everything around you. Changing your thoughts toward money involves squeezing it out and soaking up fresh and positive thoughts about wealth. Taking the list of negative ideas that you have around money, write out the opposite as affirmations. For example, if your limiting belief is 'I could never be rich because I don't deserve it' then you need to flip the script to read 'I deserve to be wealthy!'

You need to create a new message for yourself, one that says I AM ABUNDANT! The new beliefs that you are writing out will become part of your psyche and will shift your connection to money in a way that benefits you entirely. This technique enables you to rewrite and reprogram your subconscious mind to adopt a healthier attitude toward money. It will give you the fuel that you need to work toward what you want and will help you to recognize that you are meant to have all of the prosperity that you could ever dream of.

As you write out your new beliefs make sure to start your sentences with 'I am' or 'I have'. When you write in the present tense you are telling the universe that it is already happening. If the universe accepts everything that you believe to the very last detail you don't want to create affirmations that exist in the past or future as you'll be continuously waiting for them to manifest.

## IMPRESS NEW BELIEFS ONTO YOUR MINDSET

Affirmations are like building blocks that help you to create the mindset that you want. Using them can be therapeutic as you challenge old, outdated thoughts toward money, however, it can also shift your point of attraction to one that expects, loves and appreciates money. By using the affirmations that you wrote to counteract your negative beliefs you can use them to create a new ritual.

This is a crucial step as it plants the seeds of abundance and cements your new and improved relationship with money. If you remove limiting beliefs you have to replace them with exactly what will help you to consistently attract money. You want to ensure that you can continue to manifest wealth and prosperity so that you can live the lifestyle that you deserve. Positive affirmations will help you to connect to your higher power and understand the truth of your being. You were always meant to be prosperous and abundant, however, your negative experiences of money that were influenced by life events, your upbringing and other aspects have impacted your ability to attract the money you desire.

Poverty can only exist in your life if you continue to entertain thoughts of poverty. Your affirmations simply dissolve these limiting beliefs and create a fresh perspective. To use them effectively, recite your affirmations in the morning. This is when your brain is the most receptive to taking in new thoughts and ideas. It will also help you become motivated and full of the energy that you need to make your dreams come true. Using affirmations in the morning is a great way to start your day. Similarly, reading your affirmations at night will reconfigure your subconscious mind during your sleep. This is a powerful time to work with your mind and develop your thoughts and feelings toward money.

*"The first step to getting the things you want out of life is this - decide what you want."*

*Ben Stein*

# HOW TO VISUALIZE WEALTH AND ACT AS IF YOU ARE ALREADY WEALTHY

Visualization taps into the creative part of your mind. As a creator of your reality, you are using this tool every day to influence your life. When you use it in a conscious way you are deliberately inviting the money that you want to make its way toward you. Visualizing uses your imagination to focus on your goals. By creating visual sequences in your mind you tap into the energy of what you want and manifest it into your life. However, there is a particular way that can make visualization work for you. It is more than just daydreaming it uses the pure potential of the universe and harnesses the power of your mind.

If you want to manifest money, visualization can be one of the most powerful techniques that you can implement. If you can see yourself living freely with money at your disposal then you can connect with it. Visualization will free you from the confines of your current circumstances and take you to another realm where fantasy becomes reality. You can envision anything you want and tap into the feeling of happiness, bliss and joy that having the money that you want will give you. That is the magic behind visualization as it helps you to feel as though you are already wealthy.

In order to make the most out of this method, there is a secret ingredient you must use. Combined with the potential of your manifestation powers, it will almost certainly help you to attract exactly what you want. When you visualize you must always use your senses. This is absolutely vital if you want to use the law of attraction to draw the money that you want to you. During your visualization when you use your senses think about the list of things that you want to buy with this money and incorporate it into your exercise.

To visualize, close your eyes and picture yourself with the money that you want. You can imagine that it has been deposited into your bank or picture yourself spending that money. Feel the energy of your visualization from every aspect of your senses.

See the new clothes that you have bought with the money you manifested.

Hear the sound of the new car that you have bought with the money.

Feel the sand between your toes as you visualize yourself on the beach of a luxury resort.

Taste the food as you dine at a 5 star restaurant.

Smell the air in the new home that you have bought for yourself and your family.

Your senses will help your visualization to feel more real and obtainable. Once you have finished your visualization, hold on to the emotional state that it brings and use it to act as if you have already reached your financial goals. This will attract the money that you want and ensure that the universe gives you more than what you bargained for.

*"Positively and negatively, you attract what you feel, you attract who you are, you attract what you attract."*

*Denzel Washington*

# GRATITUDE

If you want more money in your life you need to appreciate what you already have. Gratitude is incredibly powerful. If you have enough of it you will be granted more money and if you do not have enough you will notice that unexpected bills and money problems will suddenly become part of your experience. The magic words 'thank you' can give you everything that you want and more. As they say, it's better to lose count while naming your blessings than to lose your blessings to counting your troubles.

When you feel as though you don't have enough money you tend to focus on it and due to the law of attraction you will attract more circumstances that take money away from you. It can feel like an endless cycle that drags you into having more issues with money. However, gratitude helps you to feel good about what you have. Whether it's your job, business or any little bit of money that comes your way, saying 'thank you' will make you feel better in the long run and consequently will manifest more reasons to be thankful.

Say 'thank you' everywhere you go and mean it. If you get a discount on something then give thanks. If you find a penny on the ground then appreciate it. When you receive your paycheck feel good because you have money coming in. Even if you don't have any money in your bank account, feel grateful for all the times that you had money in the past. There is always a reason to be grateful and your gratitude should not depend on whether or not you already have what you want.

To help you attract money and focus on the positive financial aspects in your life, start writing a gratitude list. Any time that you receive money write it out in a journal. Even when a bill comes in the post, think about the service that was available to you and feel grateful. As you slowly start to incorporate gratitude into your life you will feel better about money and you will receive more abundance in the process.

You can have as much money as your heart desires. It is up to you to create the reality that you want. You are like a magnet that attracts or repels money and so it is within your power to manifest the life that you truly deserve. Fill your life with light and love, in return, you will receive abundance and prosperity.

*"You are a magnet. Whatever you are, that's what you draw to you. If you're negative, you're going to draw negativity. If you're positive, you're going to draw positivity."*

*Steve Harvey*

# DREAM LIFE COST CALCULATOR

How much is it going to cost you to live your dream life? How much do you actually need to make to get there? If you want to live your dream life, you need to calculate how much it will cost you.

| CATEGORY | COST |
|---|---|
| HOME | |
| FOOD | |
| SHOPPING | |
| UTILITIES | |
| HOUSEHOLD | |
| TRANSPORTATION | |
| HOBBIES | |
| VACATION | |
| FITNESS/WELLNESS | |
| DINING OUT | |
| GIFTS | |
| | |
| | |
| | |
| | |
| | |

MONTHLY TOTAL.................. YEARLY TOTAL........................

# MY DREAM LIFE

## I AM ATTRACTING THE LIFESTYLE OF MY DREAMS WITH EASE AND CLARITY.

## I AM PASSIONATE.

## I AM SUCCESSFUL.

## I AM CONFIDENT.

## I AM RELENTLESS.

## I AM ABUNDANT.

THIS DREAM LIFE IS POSSIBLE FOR ME.

I EASILY ATTRACT (YOUR MONTHLY TOTAL) ______________ EVERY MONTH, THROUGH (HOW? YOUR DREAM BUSINESS / YOUR JOB)

______________________________________________.

I AM DESERVING OF RECEIVING ALL THINGS ABUNDANT IN LIFE.

I AM DESERVING OF AN AMAZING LIFE.

.............................................

YOUR SIGNATURE

# AFFIRMATIONS

If you have been reading or learning about the law of attraction for a while, then you must have come across the term "positive affirmations." Affirmations can give you a boost and help you raise your vibration, which is a required ingredient in any manifestation process or journey. Lots of people from all walks of life have benefited immensely from the efficacy of positive affirmations.

Positive affirmations are easy to use because you only have to say them repeatedly to yourself until you begin to feel their impact in your everyday life. While most people who are familiar with the concept of manifestation know what affirmations are, it's not uncommon to still find newbies struggling to put the pieces together.

Positive affirmations are extremely powerful, short statements that you can use to fire up your confidence and raise your vibration frequently. Positive affirmations can deliver extraordinary results when used the right way. And there's no better way to use them than to align your everyday life with them. You should not just say these positive affirmations as a daily ritual, they should become a part of you and before you know it, those words will start making you a better person.

Research shows that 8 out of 10 thoughts coming out of your subconscious mind are negative, can affect the kind of life you live and the things you can manifest. Positive affirmations put you in charge of your thought process and you will be able to focus only on positive things. When you consistently say these affirmations, your subconscious mind will be left with no other choice than to accept only positive vibes and free itself from all the negative thoughts.

When you form the habit of saying positive affirmations every day, you are proactively training your mind to always reject negativity and only choose positivity. Here are some examples of affirmations you can start using to align your thoughts:

- I am full of different money-making ideas.
- I am manifesting new business opportunities and concepts every day.
- I am in full control of my finances.
- I am independent and successful.
- I am a source of blessing and inspiration to the people around me.
- I am stepping into my success and greatness this week.
- I am blessed beyond every reasonable doubt.
- I am a force to be reckoned with in every of life's endeavors.
- Every move I make takes me a step closer to my goal.
- I am attracting people with high vibrational frequency.

The key to having success with affirmations is to be consistent and never go a day without saying them. To make things easier, you can adopt them as your morning ritual. You can stand in front of the mirror every morning and say the affirmations that relate to the outcome you want to manifest.

Another thing you need to know is that having the right mindset will make these positive affirmations more effective when you use them. Remember the aim is to raise your vibration and get you closer to manifesting your dream, and it's hard to achieve without the right mentality.

# AFFIRMATIONS FOR WEALTH & SUCCESS

- I am committed to my own success.
- I believe I can do anything, but fail.
- I am full of purpose, vision, and ability.
- I am worthy of the wealth I desire.
- Every goal that I set, I accomplish.
- I walk in confidence and power.
- My potential to succeed is infinite.
- I am chosen, valuable, and I always succeed.
- I can achieve greatness.
- Money flows to me effortlessly.
- My intellectual property is worth more than all the riches of the world.
- I am more than a conqueror.
- I am a magnet for success.
- I am determined to take my seat at the table.
- Winning is my birthright.
- I am financially free.
- My career is a perfect fit for me.
- I am proud of what I accomplished.
- Nothing can stop me from achieving my dreams.
- I have the courage to create positive change in my life.
- I make bold financial decisions that work in my favor.
- I always have enough money.
- I am creative in acquiring various streams of income.
- I have unlimited resources to fuel my success.
- I love money because money loves me.
- I am a money magnet.
- Success comes naturally to me.
- My net worth is growing daily.
- Wealth is pouring into my life.

# AFFIRMATIONS FOR ABUNDANCE

- My destiny is filled with abundance.
- I deserve abundance in my life.
- I am worthy of a wealthy life.
- I am opening myself to unlimited wealth.
- I can have everything I want in life.
- I am blessed. It's natural for me to feel abundant.
- I am free to create the life I desire to live.
- I am aligned with the energy of wealth and abundance.
- I am the architect of my life.
- I live a healthy, wealthy life.
- I have an abundance mindset.
- My life is abundant.
- My income is always increasing.
- I always have everything I need.
- My goals and dreams always come true.
- I am grateful for my full, rich, and prosperous life.
- I attract miracles into my life.
- Abundance comes to me easily.
- I deserve abundance and prosperity.
- Every day I am attracting wealth and abundance.
- I stand firmly in my truth and hold my head high as I boldly make my dreams my reality.
- I am financially abundant and free.
- My network is substantial and supportive.
- My income is constantly increasing.
- I am open to receiving limitless abundance.
- I get rich doing what I love.
- Abundance is all around me.
- I am generous on every occasion.
- As I give, my wealth increases.
- Abundance is my birthright.
- I was born to be abundant.

# HABITS

A habit is a pattern of behavior that is repeated on a regular basis. This behavior might take the form of action, a routine, or a way of life. What you do again and again shapes who you are.

Today, your life is simply the sum of your behaviors. As a result of your behaviors, how fit or out of shape are you? As a result of your behaviors, how successful or unsuccessful are you?

To choose which habit adjustments to undertake, first do an audit of your everyday activities. Take note of how you spend your time, energy, and attention. The most effective strategy to modify undesirable behaviors is to replace them with new ones. Begin with tiny, simple modifications that you can implement on a daily basis. Celebrate every time you succeed in your habit! Feeling happy aids your brain's ability to wire in new actions, making them more likely to be repeated automatically. Good habits to transform your life:

- Journal,
- Exercise,
- Go offline,
- Spread kindness,
- Practice gratitude,
- Eat a balanced diet,
- Drink plenty of water,
- Learn something new,
- Practice mindful living,
- Read thoughtful books,
- Use positive affirmations,
- Practice daily meditation,
- Spend some time outdoors,
- Develop a healthy sleep routine

# DESIGNING YOUR HABITS

| HABITS TO BREAK | YOUR IDEAL HABITS | WHAT WILL YOUR FUTURE SELF TELL YOU, IF YOU DON'T START WITH THIS NOW? |
|---|---|---|
| | | |
| | | |
| | | |
| | | |
| | | |

# ELIMINATE EXCUSES

Stop with the excuses - it's time to make a change. Like all bad habits, excuses are easy. They allow us to box ourselves into our comfort zone and be "okay" with our life. The excuses we use are not always something that we intentionally do. Sometimes they get the best of us, and we are not even aware of the consequences. If you want to achieve happiness in your life, and feel good with yourself, you need to stop with the excuses and start doing things instead. Become unstoppable by eliminating excuses.

| YOUR EXCUSES | WHAT YOU WILL DO INSTEAD |
|---|---|
| | |
| | |
| | |
| | |
| | |

# MONTHLY HABIT TRACKER

| MONTHLY HABIT | M | T | W | T | F | S | S |
|---|---|---|---|---|---|---|---|
| | | | | | | | |
| | | | | | | | |
| | | | | | | | |
| | | | | | | | |
| | | | | | | | |
| | | | | | | | |
| | | | | | | | |
| | | | | | | | |
| | | | | | | | |
| | | | | | | | |
| | | | | | | | |
| | | | | | | | |
| | | | | | | | |

*"In essence, if we want to direct our lives, we must take control of our consistent actions. It's not what we do once in a while that shapes our lives, but what we do consistently."*

*Tony Robbins*

# SCRIPTING

Scripting is a fun and one of the best Law of Attraction techniques out there!

Scripting is a Law of Attraction technique where you write a story about your life based on how you want it to be. This technique really gets you into character and makes your manifestation so much easier! When scripting you write story as if it has already happened, focusing on how you would feel when your desire manifested.

Rather than writing what you want to happen, you write as if it's already happening. The point is to get excited and to feel good. Close your eyes and see what you want to manifest. Visualize your dream life or goal. Imagine every aspect of your desire and see yourself with it. Try to be as specific as possible. The more you feel as if you're living it, the more excited you get and the higher your vibration will be. When you release those high vibrations, you attract them right back to you. Scripting works so well because your are not only focusing on what you want to manifest, but how it makes you feel, and showing gratitude for it.

- Use the present tense in your script. This puts the energy out that the desire you're wishing to attract is already yours - because it is! The key is to put yourself in the shoes of your future self and write from the perspective of that version of you.
- It should be explicitly clear and detailed. Don't ever be worried that you're being too detailed, the more detail you can provide the better. This clarifies your manifestations. For example, if you are trying to script your ideal home you should get as specific as possible, describing every sma

aspect of the house. That doesn't mean you should obsess or worry over the details, but more so, lay them all out.

- Record your feelings associated with manifesting. Make note of what it feels like to have it. Do you feel a sense of pride because you have achieved something? Do you feel peaceful? Do you feel immense joy?
- Additionally, don't forget to script your gratitude for having manifested your dream or goal.

Journal as if you're living that dream life, have that dream car (or whatever intention you set). Dream big! Be detailed! This is your time to really explore and journal out what reality looks and feels like! Read your script regularly and you'll bring your vibrational energy into alignment with your desires, causing them to manifest in your life.

You are the creator of your own reality. You are the writer and you can tell your story exactly as you want.

## SCRIPTING EXAMPLE

*Date Monday, July 31, 2022*

*The date is important - you will be able to go back later on and see it all manifested!*

*Write as it already happened*

*I am so happy and grateful now that I am living in abundance of great health, increasing wealth and thriving relationships. I am so grateful that I have goals to motivate me, dreams to inspire me and purpose to fuel me.*

*Life is so good right now!*

*Write in present tense*

*Thank you Universe!*

*Express gratitude*

# SCRIPT YOUR IDEAL MONTH

*Date*

*I am so happy and grateful now that*

# SCRIPT YOUR IDEAL YEAR

*Date*

*I am so happy and grateful now that*

# SCRIPT YOUR DREAM JOB

*Date*

*I am so happy and grateful now that*

# SCRIPT YOUR IDEAL PARTNER

*Date*

*I am so happy and grateful now that*

# SCRIPT YOUR DREAM HOME

*Date*

*I am so happy and grateful now that*

# SCRIPT YOUR DREAM VACATION

*Date*

*I am so happy and grateful now that*

# SCRIPT YOUR DREAM LIFE

*Date*

*I am so happy and grateful now that*

# GRATITUDE JOURNALING

Gratitude journaling is one of the most powerful manifestation exercises. The benefits and the effects are almost endless and can be felt in nearly all areas of your life. Taking the time to write down everything you are grateful for can improve your self-esteem, help you feel relaxed and sleep better, help you stay positive, make you happier, reduce stress, and help keep your vibrational frequency on a high.

Gratitude journaling becomes more fun when you make it a habit. Since you will be making daily entries for the next 4 weeks, it's good to choose a certain time when you will make your entry each day.

Gratitude is a superpower emotion, practicing gratitude on a daily basis can drastically increase your quality of life. In fact, gratitude plays a big role in every aspect of your life.

It's now time to start making your entries. There are several gratitude journal prompts that can inspire what you write in your journal every day for the next 4 weeks. You can look at some of the prompts below for ideas:

- Looking outside your window, mention some of the things you can see and are thankful for.
- Think of the unique abilities you have.
- Think about a kind gesture from a friend or loved one.
- Think of those things that put a smile on your face in the past few days
- Try to remember a particular time when you helped someone in need.

- Mention someone who once rendered unsolicited help to you.
- Be thankful for the opportunity to see another day.
- Be grateful for the gift of a strong body and mind.
- Pull out a random photo and highlight why you cherish that moment.

You can also write about your coworkers, your business or job, your favorite food, your city or neighborhood, the current season, an unexpected event that happened, etc.

At the end of the day, there are endless possibilities when it comes to finding ideas to put in your journal. Just make sure you are making at least one entry each day for the next 4 weeks and, most importantly, have fun doing it.

Here is an example:

Date: *Thursday August 17*

Today I am grateful for:

1. *Waking up this morning alive and healthy*
2. *My strong and capable body*
3. *A roof over my head*

**Highlights of the week**

*Getting a drink with an old friend*

*Doubled my previously highest weekly income*

Date: ______________________

Today I am grateful for:

..............................

..............................

..............................

Date: ______________________

Today I am grateful for:

..............................

..............................

..............................

Date: ______________________

Today I am grateful for:

..............................

..............................

..............................

Date: ______________________

Today I am grateful for:

..............................

..............................

..............................

Date:

Today I am grateful for:

Date:

Today I am grateful for:

Date:

Today I am grateful for:

Highlights of the week

Date: ______________________________

Today I am grateful for:

..............................................................................

..............................................................................

..............................................................................

Date: ______________________________

Today I am grateful for:

..............................................................................

..............................................................................

..............................................................................

Date: ______________________________

Today I am grateful for:

..............................................................................

..............................................................................

..............................................................................

Date: ______________________________

Today I am grateful for:

..............................................................................

..............................................................................

..............................................................................

Date:

Today I am grateful for:

Date:

Today I am grateful for:

Date:

Today I am grateful for:

Highlights of the week

Date: ______________________________

Today I am grateful for:

..........................................................................

..........................................................................

..........................................................................

Date: ______________________________

Today I am grateful for:

..........................................................................

..........................................................................

..........................................................................

Date: ______________________________

Today I am grateful for:

..........................................................................

..........................................................................

..........................................................................

Date: ______________________________

Today I am grateful for:

..........................................................................

..........................................................................

..........................................................................

Date:

Today I am grateful for:

Date:

Today I am grateful for:

Date:

Today I am grateful for:

Highlights of the week

Date: ______________________________

Today I am grateful for:

..........................................................................................

..........................................................................................

..........................................................................................

Date: ______________________________

Today I am grateful for:

..........................................................................................

..........................................................................................

..........................................................................................

Date: ______________________________

Today I am grateful for:

..........................................................................................

..........................................................................................

..........................................................................................

Date: ______________________________

Today I am grateful for:

..........................................................................................

..........................................................................................

..........................................................................................

Date:

Today I am grateful for:

Date:

Today I am grateful for:

Date:

Today I am grateful for:

Highlights of the week

# MORNING PAGES

We all face different challenges in our day-to-day life. We are constantly under pressure and trying to meet certain expectations. Maybe it's your bills, lover, family, school, job, or other pursuits. The bottom line is that you have a lot of things on your mind that probably keep you awake for a moment at night now and then.

Morning pages are three pages of stream-of-consciousness writing done in the morning, typically encouraged to be in longhand. Longhand means that your pages are written in your ordinary handwriting, and stream of consciousness is simply your thoughts and reactions in a continuous flow.

Morning pages are not meant to be typed, they're not meant to be strategized, and they really do serve you the best when they're done as early in the day as possible.

Write whatever comes to your mind. It's called consciousness writing after all. Find a comfortable position and start writing. The key here is ensuring you complete the three pages whether you are motivated or not. Don't worry too much about what you are writing down, you can write about anything your dreams, goals, your worries, the sky, your dog, the meal at the restaurant, and so on.

Morning pages can help you break free from all the burden weighing you down and prepare your mind to receive and achieve what you have set out to accomplish. You will be able to rise above the voice within you, especially the ones making you doubt yourself.

Date:........................................

# READ OUT LOUD

I AM CAPABLE.

I AM SUCCESSFUL.

I AM IN CHARGE OF MY LIFE.

I AM MANIFESTING MY DREAMS INTO REALITY AND CREATING THE LIFE I DESERVE TO LIVE.

# 5X55 MANIFESTATION METHOD

The 5x55 manifestation technique works by using your unconscious mind to align the vibrational frequency of your intention. It's simply done by repeating a specific affirmation 55 times for 5 consecutive days.

## THE MEANING OF 555 IN NUMEROLOGY

The significance of the number 555 in numerology is a contributing factor to the effectiveness of the 5x55 technique. If we analyze what the number 555 means in numerology, we'll realize that it contains three digits that are repeated.

The number 5 is a symbol of change, adjustment, and transformation. So, when you focus on the number 5 while trying to manifest a specific outcome, you are aligning with the sacred energy of this powerful number.

*"Man, alone, has the power to transform his thoughts into physical reality; man, alone, can dream and make his dreams come true."*

*Napoleon Hill*

## HOW TO USE THE 5X55 MANIFESTATION TECHNIQUE

This manifestation method, when done correctly, helps to influence your energy vibrations, and it can deliver fast results, which makes it one of the most popular manifestation techniques out there. This method will only take you 5 days to complete.

## STEP 1 CHOOSE AN AFFIRMATION

After you decide on the outcome you want to manifest, the next thing is to pick an affirmation that best relates to that outcome. You can only use one affirmation with this method, so you can start by writing down five affirmations and then cut it down to one.

Make sure the affirmation you choose is simple and short, but long enough to contain the specific thing you want to manifest.

Example:

*"I am grateful to the universe for sending me a check of $150."*

## STEP 2 BE IN THE RIGHT MOOD

Make sure you are in a good mood and ensure nothing disturbs you. Also, you need to choose the times on all 5 days when you will be free. You will need to allocate about 20-30 minutes each day for this exercise, although it depends on how fast you can write your affirmation 55 times.

*"If we look at the world with a love of life, the world will reveal its beauty to us"*

*Daisaku Ikeda*

## STEP 3 START WRITING

Make sure you are using a real pen, not a pencil. You will need to write down your chosen affirmation 55 times and then repeat the process for 5 consecutive days.

When witting the affirmation, it's important to stay relaxed and keep your mind fixed on the outcome you are trying to manifest. You don't want any form of distraction at these critical times. You can also say the affirmations aloud while writing.

## STEP 4 TAKE YOUR MIND OFF IT

After completing the five days of writing, you need to take your mind off the entire process and focus on something else. Don't start obsessing over the outcome you are trying to manifest as this might allow unbelief to set in. the last thing you want to be doing at this stage is worrying about when your manifestation will take place.

You want to stop thinking about the whole process. You've done your part diligently and faithfully. It's now time to leave the universe to do its part in due time. The key is to hold trust and peace to welcome anything that comes to you.

Remember:

# THE UNIVERSE ALWAYS HAS YOUR BACK!

# HAVE FAITH! TRUST! LET GO!

"You are the creator of your destiny."

DATE:

MANIFESTATION INTENTION:

1.
2.
3.
4.
5.
6.
7.
8.
9.
10.
11.
12.
13.
14.
15.
16.
17
18.
19.
20.
21.
22.
23.
24.
25.

26.
27.
28.
29.
30.
31.
32.
33.
34.
35.
36.
37.
38.
39.
40.
41.
42.
43.
44.
45.
46.
47.
48.
49.
50.
51.
52.
53.
54.
55.

# DAY 2

**DATE:**

"There is nothing you can not have."

MANIFESTATION INTENTION:

1.
2.
3.
4.
5.
6.
7.
8.
9.
10.
11.
12.
13.
14.
15.
16.
17
18.
19.
20.
21.
22.
23.
24.
25.

26.

27.

28.

29.

30.

31.

32.

33.

34.

35.

36.

37.

38.

39.

40.

41.

42.

43.

44.

45.

46.

47.

48.

49.

50.

51.

52.

53.

54.

55.

"There are no limitations."

MANIFESTATION INTENTION:

1.
2.
3.
4.
5.
6.
7.
8.
9.
10.
11.
12.
13.
14.
15.
16.
17
18.
19.
20.
21.
22.
23.
24.
25.

26.

27.

28.

29.

30.

31.

32.

33.

34.

35.

36.

37.

38.

39.

40.

41.

42.

43.

44.

45.

46.

47.

48.

49.

50.

51.

52.

53.

54.

55.

# DAY 4

"All abundance starts in the mind."

**DATE:**

MANIFESTATION INTENTION:

1.
2.
3.
4.
5.
6.
7.
8.
9.
10.
11.
12.
13.
14.
15.
16.
17
18.
19.
20.
21.
22.
23.
24.
25.

26.

27.

28.

29.

30.

31.

32.

33.

34.

35.

36.

37.

38.

39.

40.

41.

42.

43.

44.

45.

46.

47.

48.

49.

50.

51.

52.

53.

54.

55.

# DAY 5

"Your power is in your thoughts."

**DATE:**

**MANIFESTATION INTENTION:**

1.
2.
3.
4.
5.
6.
7.
8.
9.
10.
11.
12.
13.
14.
15.
16.
17
18.
19.
20.
21.
22.
23.
24.
25.

26.
27.
28.
29.
30.
31.
32.
33.
34.
35.
36.
37.
38.
39.
40.
41.
42.
43.
44.
45.
46.
47.
48.
49.
50.
51.
52.
53.
54.
55.

# ACT AS IF

Acting "as if" is one of the oldest manifestation methods and it remains one of the most effective techniques in the law of attraction. Once you master the act of "acting as if," it opens up doors of possibilities. Imagine being in a state of mind where anything is possible because you believe you can achieve whatever you focus on.

Acting "as if" simply means acting as if you already have what you are trying to manifest. While it sounds so simple to the ears, in reality, you need to take a series of proactive steps and train your mind to accept that you already have what you are trying to get from the universe.

Even if you've never come across the term "Acting as if," you've probably come across the term "fake it till you make." While faking it till you make it might not be the best way to represent "acting as if," it's the closest thing to it and the difference between the two terms lies in the mindset of the person. Both sentiments, however, have their roots in the law of attraction and the principle of manifestation, which is simply using your mind, actions, and thoughts to accomplish your dreams and fulfill your heart's desires. So, instead of expelling all your energy chasing your dream, you simply refocus that energy and begin to act like that dream has been fulfilled already.

*"I thought I was the best rapper in the world. I sat around and thought about it. Then I became Kanye West."*

*Ye West*

# CAN ACTING 'AS IF' CHANGE YOUR LIFE?

We all know that one of the main principles of the law of attraction is that once you focus all your energy and thoughts on achieving a certain goal, fulfilling your dream, or manifesting a specific outcome, you will eventually see that dream coming true before your eyes.

One of the reasons this happens is that everything in the universe is made of energy, and that includes that financial blessing, that dream car of yours, or that high-paying job you desire so much. So, when you focus on those specific things, your energy aligns with that of the universe and before you know it, the universe makes your dream come true.

You also need to understand that whatever you send into the world in the form of energy comes back to you.

So, when you start talking, acting, and carrying yourself as if you already have everything your heart desires, you will notice that those things will eventually become yours because the universe will send them your way.

Also, doing this triggers a change in your mentality and perceptions, which open up new opportunities and possibilities, and you will then notice that your dreams and aspirations become clearer. You begin to see new opportunities that your eyes were never opened to previously.

A real-life example of "acting as if" is this: let's assume you are trying to manifest a new car, you can go to a car rental and hire one for the day, or you can take a trip to the auto shop, locate your favorite car and check it out. You can sit inside, handle the steering and have a feel of the interior. That way, you are aligning your intention and vibrational frequency with that of your dream car.

# HOW TO USE THE "ACT AS IF" TECHNIQUE TO MANIFEST YOUR DESIRES

First, you need to identify how someone who has manifested what you want to achieve would behave. Take some of those behaviors and start acting that way. Perform the actions regularly with faith and belief in your heart.

Act every day as if you have already achieved the outcome you seek and watch how your perception of situations and the world around you changes.

When you are presented with a situation, you should pause and ask yourself, okay, how would someone with a positive mindset react to this? That is the simplest way you can begin to "act as if" you already are a person living with a more positive mindset. Think to yourself, how would a person with a positive outlook converse with people? How would a person with a positive mindset spend their day? And then do those things. It makes you more self-aware and able to develop an awareness of yourself in your conversations.

The key with the "act as if" method is that it is based on energy, as is all manifestation. So, essentially you are acting as if you already embody positive energy. If you embody this approach, you will find yourself with positive energy.

While acting as if you are already living your dream, it's time to also start showing it in your words. Words are powerful and you can use them to create whatever future you want for yourself.

Speak with authority and like someone who has already accomplished the specific outcome you wrote down in step 1 and you will leave the universe with no other choice than to make your dream come true.

You have to believe in the process of the massive change that is about to take place in your life.

As you act in your new role, you need to believe that what you want is already yours or, at least, that you are capable of reaching that goal. Once you start acting and believing in the energy of creation, you should see...

## YOUR DESIRES BECOMING REALITY SOON.

*"See the things that you want as already yours. Know that they will come to you at need. Then let them come. Don't fret and worry about them. Don't think about your lack of them. Think of them as yours, as belonging to you, as already in your possession."*

*Robert Collier*

# 17-SECOND MANIFESTATION TECHNIQUE

If you are looking to manifest something super specific, such as a specific amount of real spendable cash, a gadget, or a text or call from a specific person, this may be a manifestation method you want to try.

Perhaps the best thing about the 17-second manifestation is the fact it doesn't take your time; it can be completed quickly and you'll still have enough time to focus on other tasks. Just as the name implies, this technique only requires about 17 seconds of your time.

While you only require a few seconds for this technique, your concentration level needs to be high when carrying it out. Remember you only have 17 seconds, so the last thing you want in that period is some unnecessary distractions.

Before you start this manifestation method, it's important to ensure your vibrational energy is on the high side. Otherwise, you may have a hard time pulling it off successfully.

This technique is so short and effective that once you get it right, it will probably become your number one manifestation technique. That's how simple and effective it is.

*"All that we are is a result of what we have thought."*

*Buddha*

# HOW TO PERFORM THE 17-SECOND MANIFESTATION TECHNIQUE

## STEP 1 BE AS RELAXED AS POSSIBLE

You want to stay in a calm position and focus your energy on the task at hand. You also want to make sure your vibrational energy is at its highest at this point. One of the best ways to get into a relaxed mood quickly is by taking deep breaths and entering a mode of meditation.

## STEP 2 DECIDE ON THE OUTCOME YOU WANT TO MANIFEST

Take a few moments to think of the outcome you want to manifest. Since you've only got 17 seconds for this exercise, you want to be sure you are not wasting a second of that trying to decide on what you want manifest.

## STEP 3 SET YOUR TIMER FOR 17 SECONDS

Any device is fine as long as it allows you to set a timer – a phone, stopwatch, or clock. Now, while in a perfectly relaxed mood, and for the next 17 seconds, focus on the outcome you are trying to manifest.

## STEP 4

## AFFIRM THE OUTCOME TO YOURSELF REPEATEDLY DURING THOSE 17 SECONDS

For instance, if you want to manifest a financial breakthrough, you can use an affirmation like "I am stepping into financial abundance." You can end the session when the timer stops.

## STEP 5

## TAKE YOUR MIND OFF IT

This seems to be the most challenging step. After completing the 17-second exercise, you need to take your mind off everything and focus on something else. This way, you are sending a signal to the universe that you have completed your part.

*"Impossible is just a big word thrown around by small men who find it easier to live in the world they've been given than to explore the power they have to change it. Impossible is not a fact. It's an opinion. Impossible is not a declaration. It's a dare. Impossible is potential. Impossible is temporary. Impossible is nothing."*

*Muhammad Ali*

# WRITE IT DOWN

## *I AM MANIFESTING MY DREAMS INTO REALITY*

I AM

I AM

I AM

I AM

I AM

I AM

I AM

I AM

I AM

# 369 MANIFESTATION METHOD

When it comes to manifestation methods, the 369 technique is probably one of the most straightforward exercises you can do, and most importantly, it works.

The 369 manifestation technique is all about writing down your desire three times in the morning, six times in the afternoon, and nine times before retiring to your bed at night. While it may look so easy, there's a spiritual significance to the numbers 3, 6, and 9, which is what makes the method so effective.

## THE MEANING OF 369 IN NUMEROLOGY

The number comprises three digits, each having a specific meaning and significance in numerology. The number 369 carries the combined vibrational energy of the three digits.

- The number 3 is a symbol of our connection to the universe or the source of creation.
- The number 6 symbolizes our inner harmony and strength
- The number 9 stands for a new birth (releasing the life we no longer want and stepping into a new life or dimension)

## HOW TO USE THE 369 MANIFESTATION TECHNIQUE

While this step seems simple, you still need to ensure you are specific with what you are trying to manifest. So, think of what outcome you want to manifest before you even get started with this technique.

Once you've figured out your outcome, it's time to put the outcome into a powerful affirmation. For instance, if you are trying to manifest a specific amount of money, you can write something like "I am so grateful I manifested $1000 in one week." Apply the 17-second rule while writing your affirmation (it should take you at least 17 seconds to write it down because it connects your written word to the subconscious mind).

## STEP 1

Write down your affirmation three times in the morning as soon you are out of bed.

## STEP 2

Write the same affirmation six times in the afternoon.

## STEP 3

Before going to bed at night, write down the affirmation nine times.

Those are the steps outlined for you. But keep in mind that while writing your affirmations, you need to trust the universe to make it work. You can continue this method for as long as you like.

# 369

## MORNING OF __/__/__

1. ..............................................................
2. ..............................................................
3. ..............................................................

## WHAT ACTIONS WILL I TAKE TODAY TO ATTRACT IT?

1. ..............................................................
2. ..............................................................
3. ..............................................................

# READ OUT LOUD

***MY STRONGEST DESIRES ARE BEING FULFILLED NOW.***

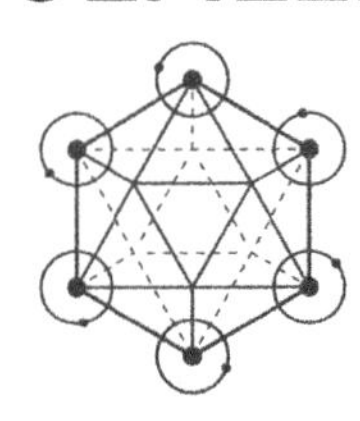

# 369

## AFTERNOON OF __/__/__

1.
2.
3.
4.
5.
6.

## NIGHT OF __/__/__

1.
2.
3.
4.
5.
6.
7.
8.
9.

# 369

## MORNING OF __/__/__

1.
2.
3.

## WHAT ACTIONS WILL I TAKE TODAY TO ATTRACT IT?

1.
2.
3.

# READ OUT LOUD

*I AM IN THE PROCESS OF BECOMING THE BEST VERSION OF MYSELF.*

# 369

## AFTERNOON OF __/__/__

1.
2.
3.
4.
5.
6.

## NIGHT OF __/__/__

1.
2.
3.
4.
5.
6.
7.
8.
9.

# 369

## MORNING OF __/__/__

1.

2.

3.

## WHAT ACTIONS WILL I TAKE TODAY TO ATTRACT IT?

1.

2.

3.

# READ OUT LOUD

***I AM VERY CLOSE TO ACHIEVING MY GOALS.***

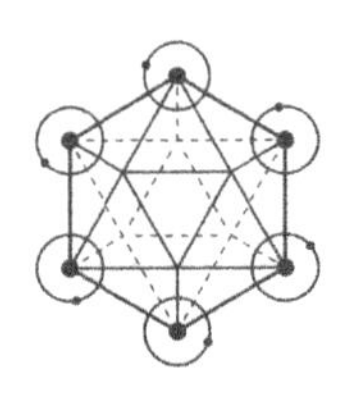

# 369

## AFTERNOON OF __/__/__

1.
2.
3.
4.
5.
6.

## NIGHT OF __/__/__

1.
2.
3.
4.
5.
6.
7.
8.
9.

# 369

## MORNING OF __/__/__

1.
2.
3.

## WHAT ACTIONS WILL I TAKE TODAY TO ATTRACT IT?

1.
2.
3.

# READ OUT LOUD

*MY WORLD CHANGES WITH MY MINDSET AND THOUGHTS.*

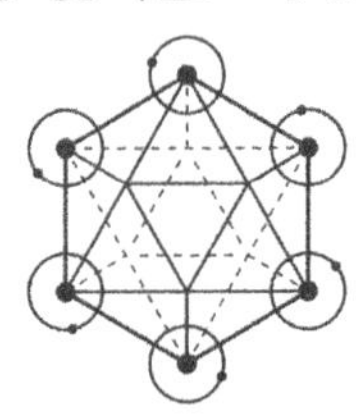

# 369

## AFTERNOON OF __/__/__

1.
2.
3.
4.
5.
6.

## NIGHT OF __/__/__

1.
2.
3.
4.
5.
6.
7.
8.
9.

# 369

## MORNING OF __/__/__

1.
2.
3.

## WHAT ACTIONS WILL I TAKE TODAY TO ATTRACT IT?

1.
2.
3.

# READ OUT LOUD

*I DESERVE TO BE SUCCESSFUL.*

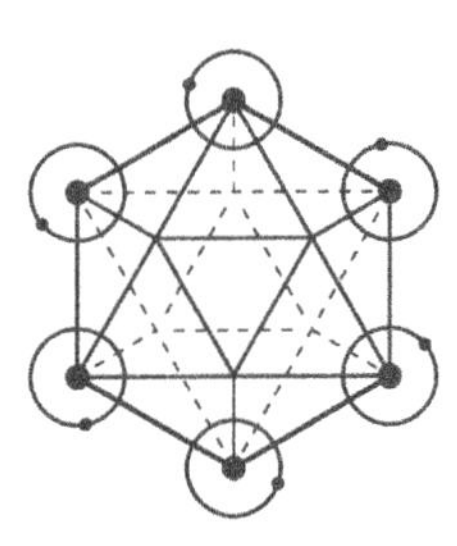

# 369

## AFTERNOON OF __/__/__

1.
2.
3.
4.
5.
6.

## NIGHT OF __/__/__

1.
2.
3.
4.
5.
6.
7.
8.
9.

# 369

## MORNING OF __/__/__

1.
2.
3.

## WHAT ACTIONS WILL I TAKE TODAY TO ATTRACT IT?

1.
2.
3.

# READ OUT LOUD

*I UNDERSTAND THAT MY ACTIONS BECOME HABITS SO I WILL ALWAYS DO THE RIGHT THINGS.*

# 369

## AFTERNOON OF __/__/__

1.
2.
3.
4.
5.
6.

## NIGHT OF __/__/__

1.
2.
3.
4.
5.
6.
7.
8.
9.

# 369

## MORNING OF __/__/__

1.
2.
3.

## WHAT ACTIONS WILL I TAKE TODAY TO ATTRACT IT?

1.
2.
3.

# READ OUT LOUD

*I HAVE A VISION AND I WORK FOR IT EVERY DAY.*

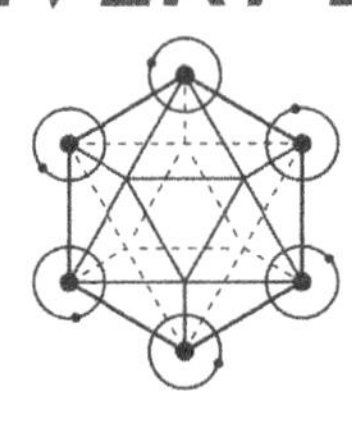

# 369

## AFTERNOON OF __/__/__

1.
2.
3.
4.
5.
6.

## NIGHT OF __/__/__

1.
2.
3.
4.
5.
6.
7.
8.
9.

# 369

## MORNING OF __/__/__

1.
2.
3.

## WHAT ACTIONS WILL I TAKE TODAY TO ATTRACT IT?

1.
2.
3.

# READ OUT LOUD

*I AM A MAGNET TO NEW OPPORTUNITIES.*

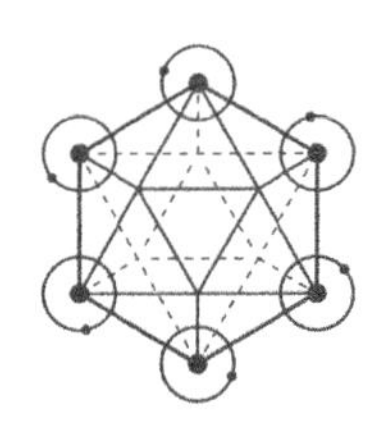

# 369

## AFTERNOON OF __/__/__

1.
2.
3.
4.
5.
6.

## NIGHT OF __/__/__

1.
2.
3.
4.
5.
6.
7.
8.
9.

# 369

## MORNING OF __/__/__

1. ..............................................................................
2. ..............................................................................
3. ..............................................................................

## WHAT ACTIONS WILL I TAKE TODAY TO ATTRACT IT?

1. ..............................................................................
2. ..............................................................................
3. ..............................................................................

# READ OUT LOUD

***I AM SATISFIED WITH WHAT I HAVE AND I'LL KEEP WORKING FOR WHAT I WANT.***

# 369

## AFTERNOON OF __/__/__

1.
2.
3.
4.
5.
6.

## NIGHT OF __/__/__

1.
2.
3.
4.
5.
6.
7.
8.
9.

# 369

## MORNING OF __/__/__

1.
2.
3.

## WHAT ACTIONS WILL I TAKE TODAY TO ATTRACT IT?

1.
2.
3.

# READ OUT LOUD

## *I AM WORTHY OF LOVE, PEACE AND HAPPINESS.*

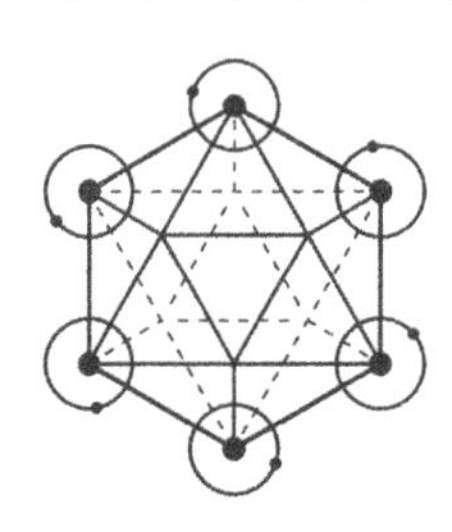

# 369

## AFTERNOON OF __/__/__

1.
2.
3.
4.
5.
6.

## NIGHT OF __/__/__

1.
2.
3.
4.
5.
6.
7.
8.
9.

YOU CAN

IF YOU

THINK

YOU CAN

# RELEASE YOUR WORRIES

Do yourself a favor and stop obsessing over things you can't control. If you're worried about anything in your life, write down everything you're worried about, then cross out the things you can't control and deal with things you can.

Remember that the only thing you can control is yourself. Decide that you'll stop obsessing over things out of your control and stick to that decision. Your body and mind will thank you.

# DECONSTRUCT YOUR PROBLEMS

Give away your problems to the Universe. Write down all your worries and problems. Visualize turning them over to the Universe. Imagine your problems are a balloon, then let it go...

Believe and trust now that the Universe will take care of all your problems. Take some time to visualize and imagine now that all is well and your life is exactly as you want it to be. Describe it and write a positive story:

..................................................

..................................................

..................................................

..................................................

..................................................

..................................................

..................................................

..................................................

..................................................

..................................................

..................................................

..................................................

..................................................

..................................................

..................................................

..................................................

..................................................

..................................................

..................................................

..................................................

Look back on it a couple of weeks or months later, and you will remember that your little problems meant nothing at all - and consequently your current big problems likely mean nothing at all in the big scheme of your life.

# FOCUS WHEEL

The objective of the focus wheel is to help raise your vibrational frequency around anything you want to manifest. It can be something general, such as seeking happiness, or something specific such as manifesting a certain amount of money.

Write your main desire in the center of the wheel, for instance," I am abundant and prosperous." Then populate the rest of the wheel with positive statements and affirmations that support that desire. Examples are "I can always afford the things I want," "I enjoy buying gifts for my friends," "Money flows to me from all directions," and so on.

Another example, if your intention is that you want to get fit you might write, going to the gym has become my regular routine., or I love and appreciate my healthy body. Then every single day, you should take the time to focus on your central intention and take the time to keep yourself focused on your goals as supported by the surrounding affirmations.

When you use the focus wheel this way, you are simply changing the vibrations surrounding your desires, which can create a surge in momentum and make it easier to achieve your manifestation.

*"Defining myself, as opposed to being defined by others, is one of the most difficult challenges I face."*

*Carol Moseley-Braun*

# EXAMPLE

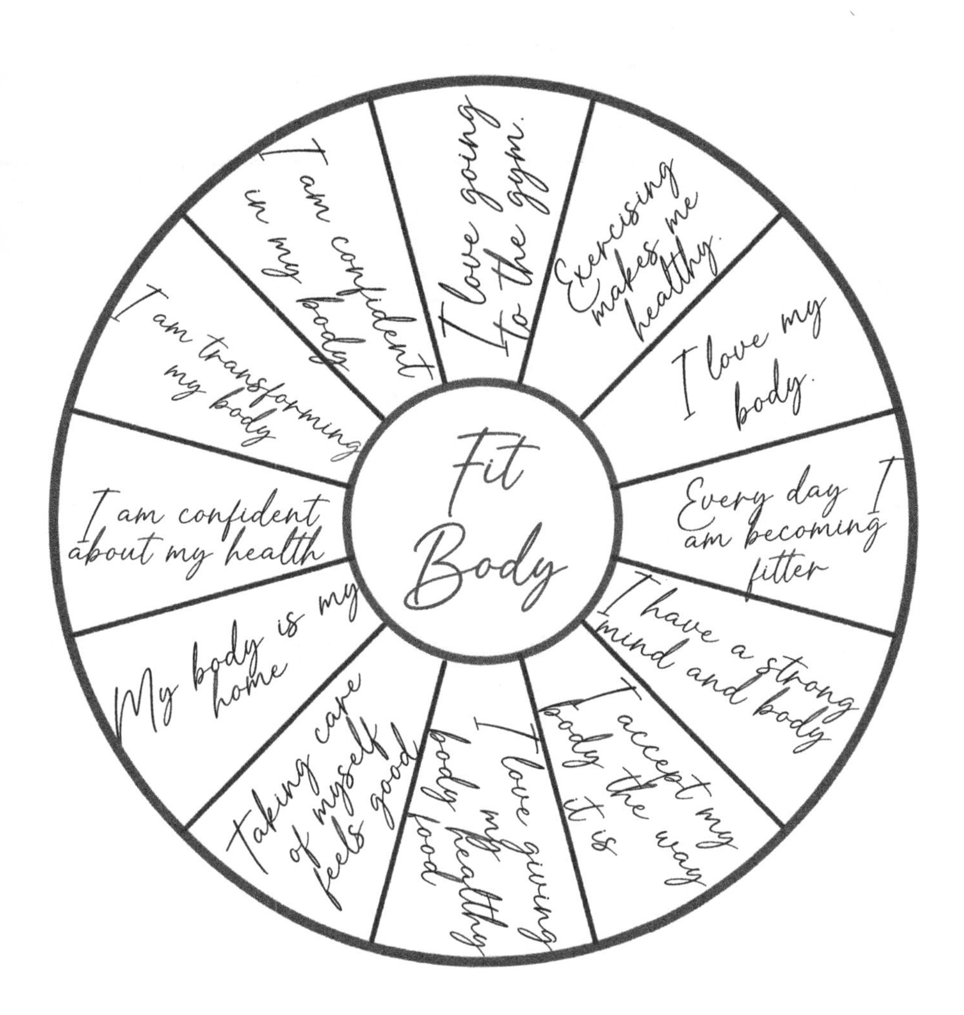


*"When you start to do the things that you truly love, it wouldn't matter whether it's Monday or Friday; you would be so excited to wake up each morning to work on your passions."*

*Edmond Mbiaka*

# CREATE YOUR OWN FOCUS WHEEL

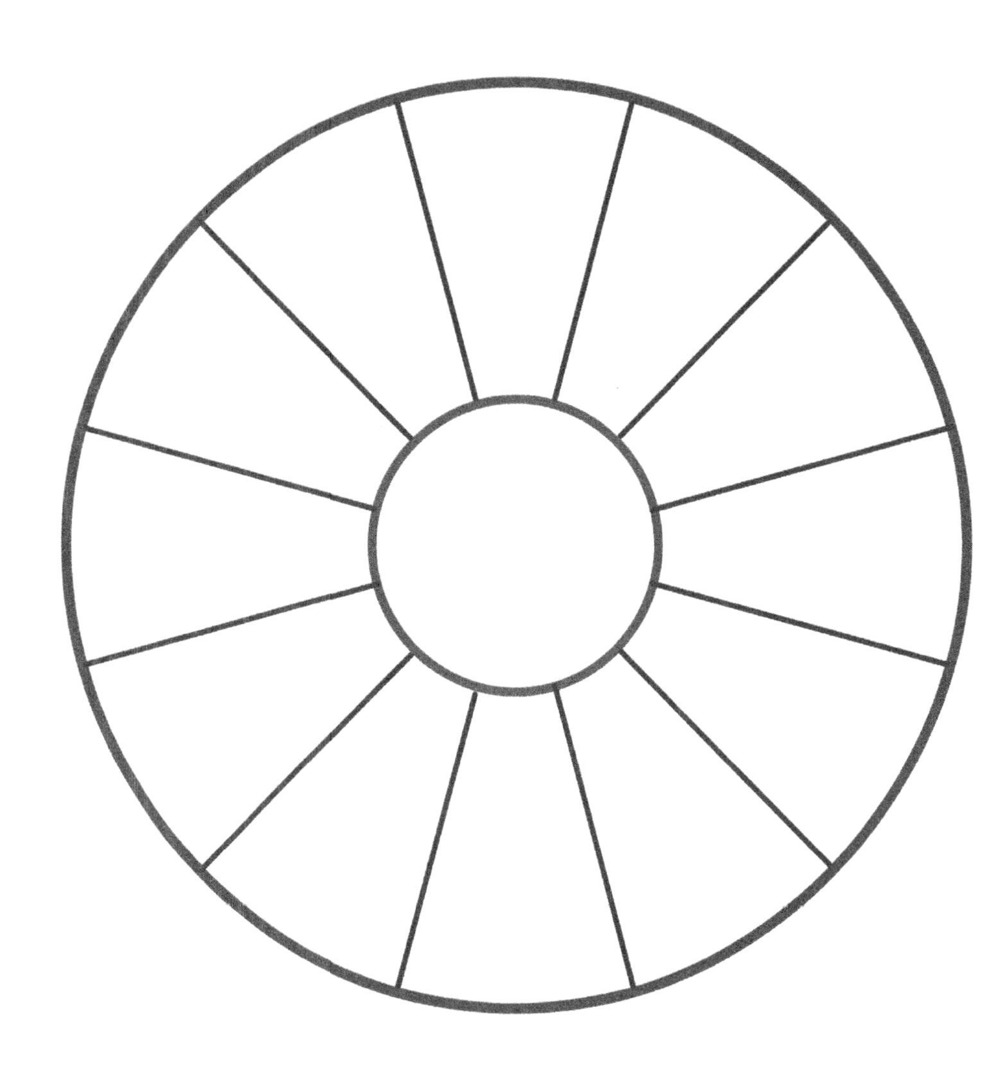

*"Every day is different, and some days are better than others, but no matter how challenging the day, I get up and live it.*

*Muhammad Ali*

# CREATE YOUR OWN FOCUS WHEEL

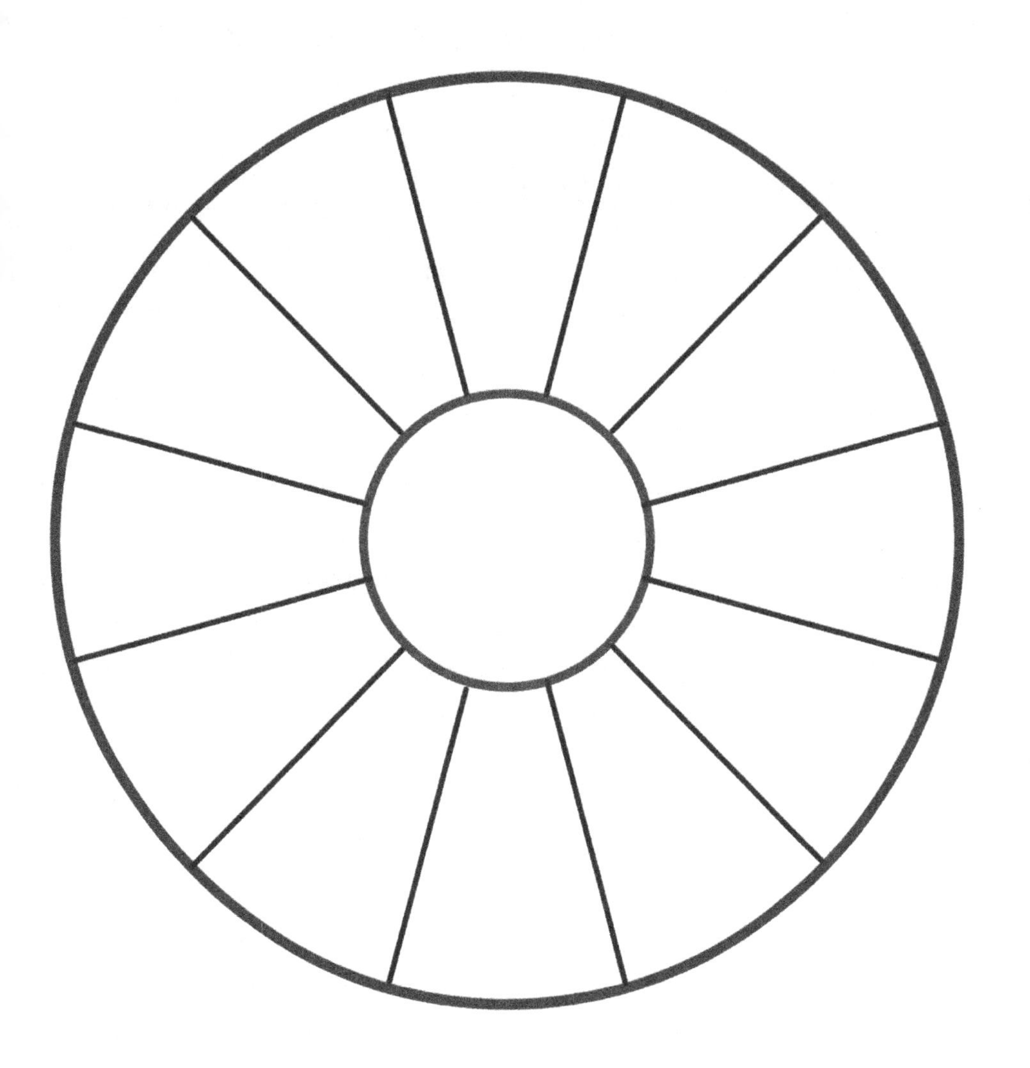

*"The chances you take, the people you meet...that's what's going to define your life"*

*Denzel Washington*

# FORGIVENESS LETTER

It's impossible to have relationships without conflicts, and when these happen there's bout to be resentments, anger, and bitterness. There are times when people will say things to you that hurts like a knife, and most of the time, conflicts are something that can have undesired effects on both parties. Both parties can feel badly hurt and hold grudges against each other.

One thing you need to realize, however, is that holding grudges and refusing to forgive someone can be counterproductive because it acts as emotional baggage that holds you down and impedes your progress. It's easy to see grudges as your way of making the other person feel bad. But in the real sense, you are hurting yourself.

Writing them a forgiveness letter sets you free and helps you find that inner peace. Before you write the letter, you want to reflect on everything that happened between you and this person. You want to think of what led to the conflict and also the role you played. Write to them letting them know you have forgiven them. In the letter, you might also want to talk about what you could have done differently. Don't forget the goal of this letter is to set get rid of the emotional baggage holding you back. After writing your letter, you don't have to send it to them. The goal is for you to find inner peace, and you've done the hard work, which is pouring out your emotions into writing.

*"It's not an easy journey, to get to a place where you forgive people. But it is such a powerful place, because it frees you."*

# I FORGIVE...

# SHADOW WORK

As you may already know, your mind is an extremely powerful tool, and it plays a vital role in shaping your present and future. While there's the conscious mind, which we are all aware of and actively make use of, there's also the subconscious mind. The latter houses your fears, worries, traits, and all the habits and information you do not want. This subconscious side is also known as the shadow.

Shadow work, when done correctly, can deliver significan physical, emotional, health, mental, and spiritual benefits. I can help improve many areas of your life and make you c better, more productive person.

Shadow work is all about tapping into the subconsciou mind, which houses all the things we run away from or hid from ourselves. Your shadow self can show up in your realit when certain triggers are pulled. And when this unconsciou side of you is awakened, you might discover some thing about your personality that deserve more of your attention.

Shadow work is all about bringing the unconscious int consciousness. It's all about bridging the gap between you conscious self and your shadow self. When you integrate th unconscious into the conscious mind, you move closer to state of complete awareness.

The more you pay close attention and accept your shado self, the more you will attain wholeness as a conscious bein and you will then have more control over various aspects c your life. Here are some shadow work prompts to help you ge started working on your shadow.

How do you feel about your childhood?
Was it generally positive or negative?
Would you describe your childhood as happy?

Recall the first time you experienced racism as a child. How did it make you feel? Does this experience still affect you as an adult? In what ways?

Which relationships in your life no longer serve you? Are you holding on to people that don't deserve your time and affections? Are you honestly happy in your relationships?

How does the weight of the generational trauma of being a black man make you feel? How does your unique trauma as a black man make you feel? How do you cope with both types of trauma?

How do you feel when you see acts of aggression or brutality against black people in the media?
How do you cope with these feelings?

# WRITE A LETTER FROM YOUR FUTURE SELF

Imagine writing to your future self 5 or 10 years from now. What would you say? What kind of person would you be? What goals would you want to have achieved? Think about what advice you want to give your future self. Doing this exercise can be an extremely insightful experience.

Date ..................................................................

# TOP PLACES I WOULD LOVE TO VISIT

1.

2.

3.

4.

5.

6.

7.

8.

9.

10.

# THE MAGIC CHECKS FROM THE UNIVERSE

The "magic check" method is a powerful and effective manifestation technique where you write a check of what you are trying to manifest, which then prompts the universe to grant your desires. Sounds simple, right? Well, that's just the simplest way to put it.

The main secret to making the magic check method work for you is gratitude. Express gratitude as though the universe already sent you the money you want. Any time you see or think about the check, be thankful as though you have received and manifested your heart desires.

The key is to have fun with it, be creative, and use it to make you feel good.

In 1985, Jim Carrey wrote himself a $10-million check for "acting services rendered," dated it 10 years in the future, and kept it in his wallet. He wrote himself a $10-million check before he had $10 million. In 1995, Carrey found out he was cast in the movie "Dumb and Dumber" for $10 million.

A coincidence? Not really.

The checks work because they already are a physical manifestation of the abundance you desire.

*"As far as I can tell, it's just about letting the universe know what you want and then working towards it while letting go of how it comes to pass."*

*Jim Carrey*

# EXAMPLE

Write your name and the value or thing you want to manifest.

Believe in it: if you order food delivery you have faith that it's going to be delivered to you, and that's exactly what you should do with the checks as well.

You can manifest more than just money. You can also manifest experiences or objects. Just write the object's/or experience's value on the check.

As an example, if you know you need $5000 to travel to Maldives, you would write $5000 on the check, and you would mention "for my dream trip".

Now that you know what abundance checks are and how to use them, we encourage you to play around with this method and have fun bringing all sorts of abundance into your life.

## HERE'S HOW YOU DO IT:

LIMITLESS ABUNDANCE
la
MANIFEST YOUR DESIRES

The Universal Bank of
Limitless Abundance

Date Enter the date

Put the amount

Pay Write down your name

To the order of How much money you would like to make

Drawer: The Universe
Account of Limitless Abundance

Signed The Universe

This is not an instrument subject to Article 3 of the UCC

You can cut them out and keep them close to you or you can put them on your vision board!

LIMITLESS ABUNDANCE
la
MANIFEST YOUR DESIRES

The Universal Bank of
Limitless Abundance

Date ____________

Pay ____________

To the order of ____________

Drawer: The Universe
Account of Limitless Abundance

Signed The Universe

This is not an instrument subject to Article 3 of the UCC


LIMITLESS ABUNDANCE
la
MANIFEST YOUR DESIRES

The Universal Bank of
Limitless Abundance

Date ____________

Pay ____________

To the order of ____________

Drawer: The Universe
Account of Limitless Abundance

Signed The Universe

This is not an instrument subject to Article 3 of the UCC

LIMITLESS ABUNDANCE
la
MANIFEST YOUR DESIRES

The Universal Bank of
Limitless Abundance

Date ____________

Pay ____________

To the order of ____________

Drawer: The Universe
Account of Limitless Abundance

Signed The Universe

This is not an instrument subject to Article 3 of the UCC

WHAT YOU IMAGINE YOU CREATE.

TRUST. HAVE FAITH. BELIEVE.

IT'S ALREADY YOURS.

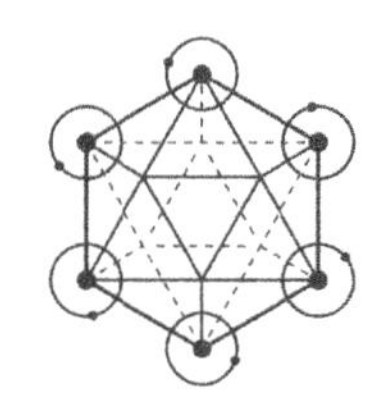

The Universe acts in mysterious ways.

The Law of Attraction is always working.

Trust the process and trust the Universe to bring you the right thing at the right time.

The day you decide that you are worthy of your dreams is the day you will start attracting and manifesting them into your life.

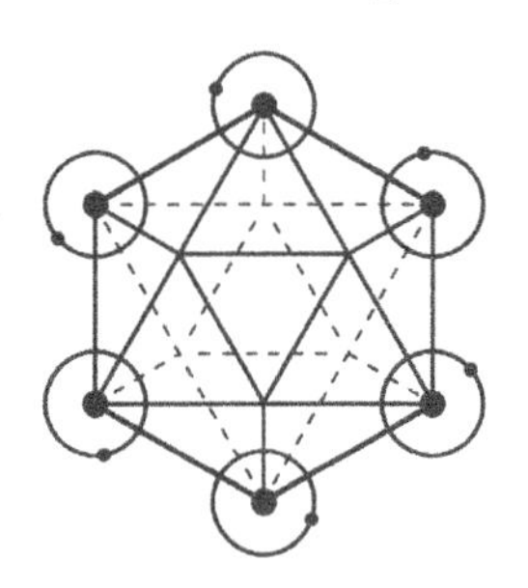

ENVISION THE FUTURE YOU DESIRE.

SEE IT. BELIEVE IT. FEEL IT

*That's all for now!*

We would love to hear from you! Your opinion matters to us! Share with us your manifestation success stories and how this journal is helping you - it will create a positive change and inspire others!

We create our journals and planners with love and great care. Yet mistakes can always happen.

For any issues with your journal, such as faulty binding, printing errors, or something else, please do not hesitate to contact us by sending us a DM on Instagram @limitlessabundance_official or email info@limitlessabundanceofficial.com

you enjoyed this journal, please don't forget to leave a review on Amazon.

*Just a simple review helps us a lot!*

Made in the USA
Las Vegas, NV
15 April 2024